The Official Offroad Camping & RVers CookBook

by
Grant Reid

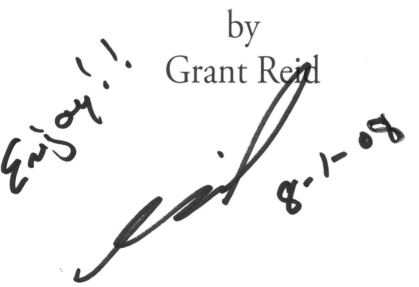

Printing in the USA by:

G&R Publishing Co.
507 Industrial Street
Waverly, Iowa 50677

ISBN 13: 978-1-4259-7036-9
ISBN 10. 1-4259-7036-2

SPECIAL THANKS

TO ALL THE ONES WHO MADE THIS BOOK POSSIBLE:

JOHN FALLS
JOHN FALLS DESIGN
(COVER DESIGN AND ILLUSTRATION)

SHEILA REID
(MARKETING)

PHILLIP DAYTON
IPS MOTORSPORTS
(FREELANCE EDITOR/PHOTOGRAPHER)

BRYAN BRACEWELL
SOUTHSIDE MARKET & BARBEQUE™
("ELGIN HOT SAUSAGE")

GIBBS & JAN GOODWIN
CHALLENGE COUNTRY
(CRAZY CRACKERS)

TERRY & JANET ESTES
MANIFOLD LUNCHES
(FUTURE TOP TRUCK CHAMPION)

THE KRUSES
ZIPPER-STYLE OMELET
(KATEMCY OFF-ROAD PARK, MASON, TEXAS)

AND MOST OF ALL!!!!!

MY FAMILY
CHRISTI, JOSH & SAMANTHA
FOR HAVING TO SAMPLE, NOT ONE, BUT ALL
OF THE TEST RECIPES.

I LOVE Y'ALL.

HINT: Don't let the dutch oven scare you. Just follow the E-Z Cooking Dutch Oven Tips.

TIP: Try these recipes before your next outing in the comfort of your home or backyard.

INTRODUCTION

The Official Off-Road, Camping and RV'ers Cookbook is structured so that one can prepare super E-Z lip-smacking finger-licking meals in less than one hour (including prep time). There are two ways to prepare each of the recipes in this cookbook (well, most of the recipes). You will find many hints and tips within the pages of this cookbook that will not only help you cook, prepare, and pre-prep your meals in the easiest fashion ever, but will also make you laugh out loud. Most of all, you will be able to treat your family or companions to four- and five-star meals (well, almost) but will also have ample time left to have what you came for, FUN! For the recipes for the off-roader and camper (tent or truck) -style cooking, you will need one of the following: dutch oven (recommended), campfire, or camp stove, and a few items on the following page, most of which you should already have. Now the RV'ers, well, you guys should have everything on board that you will need, and hey, please NO CAMPFIRES in your RV.

What are you waiting for? Let's get cooking!

HINT: Please use name-brand zipper-style bags, as generics don't hold liquids well.

TIP: When preparing recipes that require the zipper-style bags to be heated in boiling water, use freezer-style bags. They are a little thicker and will not melt or puncture.

PRE-PREP & "DINNER-IN-A-BAG®" CONCEPT

The pre-prep and "Dinner-in-a-Bag®" concept allows the person or persons cooking and prepping the meals to also have ample time to have fun, just like you and me. Camping and RVing lets you enjoy and relax in the outdoors on your time away from the everyday hustle and bustle. All the meals and recipes in this cookbook will allow you to do all the prep work at home the day or night before you leave for your outing. Okay, I know what you're thinking: There is so much to do, I will not have time. (Not true.) For the most part, short trips (weekend camping) you will only be having about two dinners, two breakfasts, and one lunch. Go through the cookbook and pick out a few recipes that will be E-Z for YOU to prep and cook. (This is the best way to start. Rome wasn't built in a day.) Once you have done that, it should only take about thirty minutes to one hour to prep the entire menu for the weekend outing. I know it's starting to sound doable, but wait, it gets E-Zer. As you are prepping, different recipes call for different ingredients to be added at different times. This is where the bag concept comes in. After cutting, chopping, rolling, slicing, measuring, and mixing spices, put each individual ingredient into small zipper-style bags. (Come on, people, no generic bags please; they do not hold liquids well.) Once you have completed that, then take all the bags for that meal and store them in a large zipper-style bag and write with a Sharpie the meal that is in that bag. (This bag will be used again later for leftovers.) The bags make for E-Z distribution and toss-in-the-trash cleanup at camp.

Definition: The words "Group and Label" mean to gather all ingredients for one meal and place together in one large zipper-style bag and label with a Sharpie the meal that's in that bag.

HINT: If you were going to go out and purchase this whole list, it would be pretty pricey. So start slow and only buy what you don't already have, and purchase only the items that you will need for your next outing.

TIP: Sit down and hang on. You are getting ready to experience the wildest and best time cooking you will ever have anywhere.

OFF-ROAD & RV'ERS COOKING LIST

Dutch oven (12" recommended); this is by far the best and E-Zest way to prepare excellent meals in less than one hour with little to no maintenance. Read and follow the E-Z dutch oven cooking methods, for flawless dutch oven cooking and tremendous compliments.

- Camp stove (one- or two-burner)
- Wooden spoons (3)
- Hot mitts or oven gloves (2)
- Medium fry pan (skillet) (1)
- Sharp knife (1)
- Spatula (1)
- Long metal tongs (1)
- Long grilling fork (1)
- Plastic measuring cup (two-cup)
- Gas for stove
- Kingsford charcoal for dutch oven
- Starter fluid (chimney starter recommended)
- Dish soap and double-sided sponge
- Paper plates
- Paper towels
- Plasticware or silverware (fingers work well when camping)
- Zipper-style bags (for leftovers)
- Foil

HINT: When choosing a dutch oven, whether small or large, choose one with a concave lid, as the recipes in this cookbook require coals on top and bottom for a wide range of cooking (bake, roast, broil, simmer).

TIP: By reading and following the E-Z cooking dutch oven tips in this cookbook, it will help you prepare each recipe with ease and confidence. Have fun!

E-Z COOKING DUTCH OVEN TIPS

There are a lot of you out there who are thinking dutch oven? *That is the way they cooked in the olden days. It can't be easy.* Well, I'm here to tell you that this is the reason that they used the dutch oven methods back in the "olden days," because it was E-Z! There is not many ways to cook outdoors that are not a pain in the backside. Well, between this cookbook and the trusty old dutch oven, your pain will be replaced with happy campers (literally) and you too will be a happy camper.

All of the recipes in this cookbook were tested in 12" Lodge Cast Iron Mfg. dutch ovens, using Kingsford charcoal briquettes. Kingsford works the best, because every briquette is virtually the same and very tightly packed to prevent popping and cracking. Match Light brands tend to burn very hot and not for very long, resulting in burned, uncooked food. Regulating oven temperature is by far the hardest thing to do, and the hints and tips below should and will help with this. For the most part, the recipes in this cookbook will be cooked at 350 degrees. As a rule of thumb, take the size of your oven in inches and multiply it by two, and that is the number of briquettes you will use.

You must rotate the dutch oven as instructed in the recipes of this cookbook to prevent hot spots, resulting in burned food. The best way to rotate the dutch oven is to place the number that is stamped on the lid in the position that you walk up to mainte-nance the dutch oven. Using hot mitts and tongs, lift lid and do not rotate, them grab the handle on the dutch oven rotating 180 degrees (that's half of a full turn). Replace lid.

EXAMPLE: If you have a 12" Lodge dutch oven and are cooking chicken cordon bleu with potatoes and broccoli for 40 minutes at 350 degrees, you would want 24 total briquettes. 12" oven x 2 = 24 bri-quettes. Use this calculation throughout this book and I will note when and how many briquettes you will need to increase the temper-atures if needed for certain recipes. For those of you cooking above 5000 feet sea level, I have found that multiplying the total number of briquettes by 24 percent will provide the right amount of heat.

Question: *Where do I put the briquettes? How many on the lid? How many underneath?* Well, here's your answer... Food to be simmered: soups, chilis, stews, etc. put one-third of the total briquettes on the lid and two-thirds of the total underneath the oven. Food to be baked: breads, rolls, biscuits, cakes, cobblers (rising), put two-thirds of the total briquettes on the lid and one-third underneath the oven. Food to be roasted: meats, chicken, casseroles, veggies, cobblers (non-rising) use half the briquettes on the bottom and half on the lid.

Remember, take it easy on the heat and follow the above sugges-tions. No one likes burned food. (Well, maybe some.)

FAVORITE RECIPES

NAME OF RECIPE	PAGE

HINT: Check out the easy sausage gravy recipe in the Side Dish Section; very easy pre-prep to be so good. Use a pat of butter on top of each biscuit.

TIP: After folding in all ingredients in mixing bowl, sprinkle a little flour over top of dough and on surface. Spread dough out using fingers (no rolling pin). Use a mayo lid to cut out biscuits.

BISCUITS
(SAUSAGE GRAVY RECIPE IN SIDE DISH SECTION)

OFF-ROAD & CAMPING STYLE

INGREDIENTS
2 cups self-rising flour
1 cup milk
1 tbsp. mayo (buttermilk flavor)
1 tbsp. oil

TOOLS
dutch oven
charcoal
lighter fluid
hot mitts
med. mixing bowl
fork

Pre-prep: Place flour in a zipper-style bag, milk in a zipper-style bag, and mayo in zipper-style bag. Group and label.

Cooking method: Dutch oven. Use 1/3 briquettes on bottom and 2/3 briquettes on the lid. Place all ingredients in medium mixing bowl. Knead with fork until well-mixed (do not overknead; biscuits will be tough). Sprinkle flour over dough and on surface. Flatten out dough using fingers (don't use rolling pin). Using mayo lid, cut out biscuits and place in oiled dutch oven. Cook 15-20 minutes, rotating every 10 minutes until golden brown.

RV'ERS STYLE

TOOLS
med. mixing bowl
fork
baking pan
oven @ 350 degrees

Camp-prep: Place all ingredients in medium mixing bowl. Knead with fork until well-mixed (do not overknead; biscuits will be tough). Sprinkle flour over dough and on surface. Flatten out dough using fingers (don't use rolling pin). Using mayo lid cut out biscuits and place on oiled baking pan.

Cooking method: Oven at 350 degrees. Place biscuits in oven for 15 minutes or until golden brown. Enjoy.

Bonus: Garlic and Cheese Biscuits; Cut the mayo and add 1 tbsp minced garlic and 2/3 cup grated cheddar cheese. Prep and cook methods are the same. Enjoy.

HINT: Real men don't eat quiche, so I have named this one "Redneck Breakfast." This way, they can tell all their buddies that they had a redneck breakfast, and have no idea it is just another name for quiche.

TIP: This is a feed-everyone-size recipe. For four people, I would say to cut this recipe in half unless you are planning on having Redneck Breakfast Burritos for lunch. (See Manifold Lunches.)

REDNECK BREAKFAST

OFF-ROAD & CAMPING STYLE

INGREDIENTS
1 lb. bacon
1/2 lb. sausage
2 med. onions
1 1/2 fresh mushrooms
1 green bell pepper
3 tbsp. garlic

1 lb. of diced frozen
   hash brown potatoes
12 eggs
3 cups Monterey/
   cheddar cheese
salt and pepper (to taste)
1 tbsp. oil

TOOLS
dutch oven
charcoal
lighter fluid
hot mitts
spoon

Pre-prep: Slice bacon into 1" pieces and microwave until slightly crispy. Cook sausage on stovetop. Drain fat and set aside. In medium bowl, beat eggs. Add bacon, sausage, and 1 cup cheese to eggs. Stir. Place in zipper-style bag. Dice onions and green pepper. Slice mushrooms. Sauté onions, mushrooms, green pepper, and garlic for 5 minutes. Stir in potatoes. Add salt and pepper. Cook for 15 min. or until potatoes are brown and tender. Let cool. Place in _____ (fill in blank) style bag. Leave remaining cheese in bag. Group and label.

Cooking method: Dutch oven. Use 1/3 briquettes on bottom and 2/3 briquettes on the lid. Add oil and potato mixture to dutch oven. Pour egg mixture over potatoes. Cook 30 minutes, rotating every 10 min. Sprinkle remaining cheese on top and cook until cheese is melted or until eggs are set (5-10 minutes). Enjoy!

RV'ERS STYLE

TOOLS
stovetop med. to medium-high heat
large skillet
medium bowl
spoon

Camp-prep: Slice bacon into 1" pieces and microwave until slightly crispy. Dice onions and green pepper. Slice mushrooms. In medium bowl, beat eggs. Add 1 cup cheese to eggs and stir.

Cooking method: Stovetop, medium to medium-high heat. In large skillet, cook sausage. Drain fat. Stir sausage and bacon into eggs. Set aside. In same skillet, sauté onions, mushrooms, green pepper, and garlic for 5 minutes. Stir in potatoes. Add salt and pepper. Cook 15 minutes or until potatoes are brown and tender. Pour egg mixture over eggs. Cover and continue cooking about 15 minutes. Sprinkle remaining cheese on top and cook until cheese is melted or until eggs are set. Enjoy!

HINT: If you're going to be with family or friends on your next outing, when planning, if I were you, I would think about doubling this recipe, because these things will go quick and I mean quick.

TIP: After the piglets are finished cooking, don't say a word about them being done until you have set four or five aside for yourself, because I'm not kidding, they really do go fast.

FRENCH BREAD PIGLETS

OFF-ROAD & CAMPING STYLE

INGREDIENTS
french bread loaf (Poppin' Fresh
  in a can)
mini beef sausage (Lil' Smokies)

TOOLS
dutch oven
charcoal
hot mitts
knife

Camp-prep: This is a very E-Z crowd pleaser and works for breakfast, lunch, or a snack. Open the french bread tube. Leaving the loaf round, cut half-inch pieces so that you have what looks like an ordinary biscuit. (By the way, biscuits will work, but do not taste the same and aren't as good as the french loaf). Place a sausage in each one of the pieces of french loaf and fold over, mashing the edges so that it does not come open. (Now it looks like a kolache, which is what we are after.)

Cooking method: Dutch oven. Use 1/3 briquettes on the bottom and 2/3 briquettes on the lid, place all piglets in the ungreased dutch oven. Rotating every 5 minutes to prevent hot spots. Cook 20 to 25 minutes or until top is golden brown. Enjoy.

RV'ERS STYLE

TOOLS
oven @ 400 degrees
cookie sheet (ungreased)
hot pad holder

Camp-prep: This is a very E-Z crowd pleaser and works for breakfast, lunch, or a snack. Open the french bread tube. Leaving the loaf round, cut half-inch pieces so that you have what looks like an ordinary biscuit. (By the way, biscuits will work, but do not taste the same and aren't as good as the french loaf). Place a sausage in each one of the pieces of french loaf and fold over, mashing the edges so that it does not come open. (Now it looks like a kolache, which is what we are after.)

Cooking method: Oven @ 400 degrees. Place piglets on cookie sheet and toss in the oven. Bake 15 to 20 minutes or until golden brown. Enjoy.

HINT: The kids will love this one, and you better have a couple yourself, because when they finish with this one, they will be wound up tight like a rubber band.

TIP: Try this one at home for sleepovers, but wait one hour before your child's friend is to be picked up. This way, you only have one wound-up rubber band to deal with.

PECAN STICKY ROLLS

OFF-ROAD & CAMPING STYLE

INGREDIENTS
1 tube cheap-o biscuits
1/2 cup brown sugar
1/2 cup butter (1 stick)
1 cup diced pecans
3/4 tsp. cinnamon
1 tbsp. water

TOOLS
dutch oven
charcoal
charcoal starter
hot mitts
camp stove
med. skillet

Camp-prep: Camp stove at medium to medium-high heat. Cut biscuits into quarters and place in dutch oven. Using skillet, melt butter. Stir in brown sugar, cinnamon, and water. Bring to boil and reduce heat quickly, stirring constantly until it becomes caramelized. Add pecans. Pour over biscuits.

Cooking method: Dutch oven. Use 1/3 briquettes on the bottom and 2/3 briquettes on the lid. Cook 15-20 minutes or until golden brown, rotating every 5 minutes.

RV'ERS STYLE

TOOLS
oven @ 350 degrees
round 9" baking pan
stovetop, med. to med.-high heat
med. skillet

Camp-prep: Stovetop, medium to medium-high heat. Cut biscuits into quarters and place in baking pan. Using skillet, melt butter. Stir in brown sugar, cinnamon, and water. Bring to boil and reduce heat quickly, stirring constantly until it becomes caramelized. Add pecans. Pour over biscuits.

Cooking method: Oven @ 350 degrees for 10-15 minutes or until golden brown. Enjoy!

HINT: I guess I need to write a sleepover cookbook. This is a fun one to let the kids make on their own (under adult supervision) and pop it in the micro.

TIP: You can precook several different choices — bacon, sausage, ham, veggies, grated cheese, etc. and place in bowls. Let everyone shake their own egg and build their own omelet.

OMELET IN A BAG

OFF-ROAD & CAMPING STYLE

INGREDIENTS
8 eggs
pinch "o" salt
pinch "o" pepper
bacon
ham
veggies
cheese
and whatever else you can come up with
    (leftovers work well).
8 cups water

TOOLS
zipper-style freezer bag (sandwich size).
medium soup pot
campstove

Pre-prep: In each zipper-style freezer bag, place 2 eggs (my cookbook editor wants to make sure you crack the eggs before placing them in the bag, no shells.) Zip and shake well. Open and throw whatever it is you're going to use (bacon, green peppers, and cheese) and close. Group and label. Get ready for this outing, because this is cool stuff.

Cooking method: Campstove, high heat. In medium soup pot, boil water, and I mean boil (keep the water boiling). Throw the bags in and cook for 121/2 minutes exactly; pull out, open bag, and it falls right out. It really works; trust me on this one.

RV'ERS STYLE

TOOLS
zipper-style freezer bag (sandwich size).
microwave

Camp-prep: In each zipper-style freezer bag, place 2 eggs (my cookbook editor wants to make sure you crack the eggs before placing them in the bag, no shells.) Zip and shake well. Open and throw whatever it is you're going to use (bacon, green peppers, and cheese) and close.

Cooking method: Microwave on high. Place zipper-style freezer bag in micro and check it out. Cook for 2-3 minutes. (Microwaves vary in power so keep an eye on it) until set. Open and pour it out on a plate. Enjoy!

NOTES

21

HINT: Pick out jalapenos that are large in size for two reasons: One, they will be easier to stuff and you can use a whole piece of bacon, and two, you get more bang per bite.

TIP: When you first put them on the grate, place the open side of the pepper down so the bacon can cook before the cream cheese gets hot and starts to melt. This will take about 15 minutes or till the bacon is to your likin'.

GRILLED STUFFED JALAPENOS

OFF-ROAD & CAMPING STYLE

INGREDIENTS
6 large jalapeno peppers
12 strips uncooked bacon
4 oz. cream cheese
shrimp? by all means

TOOLS
spoon
toothpicks
tongs
grill/ grate/ campfire

Pre-prep: Start by cutting the peppers in half the long way so that when you finish, you have sort of a boat. Remove all of the seeds (for hot-hot, leave a few). Using a spoon, fill the boat with cream cheese so that it is crowned at the top and full. (If using shrimp, de-vein and place shrimp on top of cream cheese). Once you have stuffed all the peppers, grab the toothpicks and wrap each pepper with one slice of bacon. Use toothpicks to secure bacon. When completed with that, store in zipper-style bag and ice or refrigerate until ready to cook.

Cooking method: Campfire (recommended) or BBQ grill. Place grate over medium to hot coals for 30-40 minutes or until bacon is crisp.

RV'ERS STYLE

TOOLS
spoon
toothpicks
hot pad holder
cookie sheet/
oven @ 350 degrees

Pre-prep or camp-prep: Start by cutting the peppers in half the long way so that when you finish, you have sort of a boat. Remove all of the seeds (for hot-hot, leave a few). Using a spoon, fill the boat with cream cheese so that it is crowned at the top and full. (If using shrimp, de-vein and place shrimp on top of cream cheese). Once you have stuffed all the peppers, grab the toothpicks and wrap each pepper with one slice of bacon. Use toothpicks to secure bacon. When completed with that, store in zipper-style bag and ice or refrigerate until ready to cook.

Cooking method: Oven @ 350 degrees or BBQ grill, place peppers about 1" apart and cook for 30 to 40 minutes or until bacon is crisp.

HINT: This recipe is really fun anywhere — camping, sleepovers at home, fishing trip, etc., and gets laughs from everyone, well everyone except one, and that's the one who gets the surprise.

TIPS: Make sure you keep your eye on this one. I have found that if you put the surprise on the outside edge and roll a little pinch of dough, just stick it on the surprise ball so it will not be so obvious.

MYSTERY BALLS, BISCUITS W/ A SURPRISE

OFF-ROAD & CAMPING STYLE

INGREDIENTS
tube "O" biscuits (10 count, cheap)
cheese (of your choice)
hot dogs (cut into 1/2" pieces)
preserves (sweet tooth)
cream cheese (with dash of A1)
peanut butter & jelly
and what ever else you can think up!
1 tbsp. oil

TOOLS
dutch oven
charcoal
hot mitts
knife
cold beverage
sense of humor

Pre-prep: Start by deciding what you want in your Mystery Balls, then cut, slice, or divide the ingredients and put them into separate bags. The biscuits will be stuffed at camp by flattening the biscuits so that they are about 2" in diameter. Place the surprise in the center and close and mash edges so that it does not come open; this side will go against the bottom of the oven. Here is where the surprise part comes in: One of the biscuits you are going to stuff with something not so good, but edible (like mayo!) when served, watch the face on the person who gets this one.

Cooking method: Dutch oven. Use 1/3 briquettes on the bottom and 2/3 briquettes on the lid. Oil dutch oven well. Place Mystery Balls in bottom of dutch oven. Rotate oven every 5 minutes to prevent hot spots (see dutch oven tips). Cook 15 to 20 minutes or until brown. Serve with a smile.

RV'ERS STYLE

TOOLS
oven @ 350 degrees
cookie sheet
hot pad holder
cold beverage

Pre-prep or Camp-prep: Start by deciding what you want in your Mystery Balls, then cut, slice, or divide the ingredients and put them into separate bags. The biscuits will be stuffed at camp by flattening the biscuits so that they are about 2" in diameter. Place the surprise in the center and close and mash edges so that it does not come open; this side will go against the bottom of the oven. Here is where the surprise part comes in: One of the biscuits you are going to stuff with something not so good, but edible (like mayo!) when served, watch the face on the person who gets this one.

Cooking method: Oven @ 350 degrees. Oil cookie sheet well. Place Mystery Balls on cookie sheet. Slide into oven and cook 15 to 20 minutes or until golden brown. Serve with a smile.

25

HINT: You will want to go visit your closest RV'er friend and offer them a few stuffed mushrooms. Why, you might ask? Because later on, when you cook the quick apple/cherry/blueberry cobbler, just maybe they will offer up some ice cream. If you're in an RV, keep them all to yourself and look out for off-roaders and campers with *The Official Off-Road, Camping, & RV'ers Cookbook*.

TIP: For those of you pre-prepping this recipe try to schedule it in the first part of your outing. After the end of the second day, the mushrooms will start to become soft and mushy.

BAKED STUFFED MUSHROOMS

OFF-ROAD & CAMPING STYLE

INGREDIENTS
12 medium mushrooms
1 tbsp. olive oil
2 tbsp. minced onions
1 tsp. minced garlic
3 oz. country sausage
1 pinch "o" pepper
2 pinches "o" salt
1 tbsp. breadcrumbs
1/4 c. parmesan cheese (grated)
3 tbsp. butter

TOOLS
dutch oven
wooden spoon
knife
charcoal
charcoal starter

Pre-prep: Brush off mushrooms and remove stems. Finely chop stems (1/4 cup). Place mushroom caps in a bowl and toss with 1 tbsp. oil. Arrange caps cavity-side up. Set aside. Brown sausage in skillet. Make sure that you chop sausage as small as possible. Add onion, garlic, mushroom stems, salt, and pepper. Sauté for about 4 minutes. Remove from heat. Add cheese and breadcrumbs. Stir. Stuff mushroom caps with sausage mixture. Place in zipper-style bag and label.

Cooking method: Dutch oven. Use 1/3 briquettes on the bottom and 2/3 briquettes in the lid. Place stuffed mushrooms in dutch oven. Cook 20-30 minutes or until mushrooms are tender and cheese is slightly brown, rotating every 10 minutes.

RV'ERS STYLE

TOOLS
medium skillet
cookie sheet
hot pad holder
knife
wooden spoon
oven @ 400 degrees

Pre-prep or Camp-prep: Brush off mushrooms and remove stems. Finely chop stems (1/4 cup). Place mushroom caps in a bowl and toss with 1 tbsp. oil. Arrange caps cavity-side up on foil. Set aside. Brown sausage in skillet. Make sure that you chop sausage as small as possible. Add onion, garlic, mushroom stems, salt, and pepper. Sauté for about 4 minutes. Remove from heat. Add cheese and breadcrumbs. Stir. Stuff mushroom caps with sausage mixture. Place on cookie sheet.

Cooking method: Oven @ 400 degrees. Place cookie sheet in oven and bake for 10-15 minutes, until mushrooms are tender and cheese is slightly brown.

27

HINT: Change it up a little and try BBQ sauce instead of pizza sauce with chicken (precooked) as your topping. Or pesto sauce in place of pizza sauce with tomato and onion as your topping.

TIP: If for some reason you're somewhere campfires are not allowed, you can use a camp-stove and skillet (4 minutes on each side) and achieve similar results, but nowhere near the fun of doing them on an open fire.

PITA PIZZA

OFF-ROAD & CAMPING STYLE

INGREDIENTS   TOOLS
sourdough pita bread   knife
pizza sauce (choice)   alum. foil
mozzarella cheese   campfire
pepperoni (topping of choice)   spoon
   precooked

Pre-prep: Take your pita bread and slice it in half so that you have two round mini-pizzas. Using a spoon, put a fair amount of sauce on the pita and spread around, then the cheese on top of the sauce, and that's right, you're ready for the topping of your choice (precooked) on the cheese. Once you have done all four, wrap them separately in tight foil, store in a large zipper bag, and ice or refrigerate until ready to cook.

Cooking method: Campfire – remove pizzas from plastic bag and throw into campfire, topping-side down to start for 11/2 minutes; turn over for 11/2 minutes longer, remove from campfire, and voila, you have a quick and E-Z pizza!

RV'ERS STYLE

TOOLS
oven @ 400 degrees
foil
spoon

Pre-Prep or Camp-Prep: Take your pita bread and slice it in half so that you have two round mini-pizzas. Using a spoon, put a fair amount of sauce on the pita and spread around, then the cheese on top of the sauce, and that's right, you're ready for the topping of your choice (precooked) on the cheese. Once you have done all four, wrap them separately in tight foil, store in a large zipper bag, and ice or refrigerate until ready to cook.

Cooking method: Oven @ 400 degrees. Place foil-wrapped pizza in oven for 7 to 10 minutes, remove, and serve.

HINT: If your going to be with family or friends on your next outing, when planning, if I were you, I would think about doubling this recipe because these things will go quick and I mean quick.

TIP: After the piglets are finished cooking, don't say a word about them being done until you have set four or five aside for yourself, because I'm not kidding, they really do go fast.

FRENCH BREAD PIGLETS

OFF-ROAD & CAMPING STYLE

INGREDIENTS
french bread loaf (Poppin' Fresh
  in a can)
mini beef sausage (Lil' Smokies)

TOOLS
dutch oven
charcoal
hot mitts
knife

Camp-prep: This is a very E-Z crowd pleaser and works for breakfast, lunch, or a snack. Open the french bread tube. Leaving the loaf round, cut half-inch pieces so that you have what looks like an ordinary biscuit. (By the way, biscuits will work, but do not taste the same and aren't as good as the french loaf). Place a sausage in each one of the pieces of french loaf and fold over, mashing the edges so that it does not come open. (Now it looks like a kolache, which is what we are after.)

Cooking method: Dutch oven. Use 1/3 briquettes on the bottom and 2/3 briquettes on the lid, place all piglets in the ungreased dutch oven. Rotating every 5 minutes to prevent hot spots. Cook 20 to 25 minutes or until top is golden brown. Enjoy.

RV'ERS STYLE

TOOLS
bake @ 400 degrees
cookie sheet (ungreased)
hot pad holder

Camp-prep: This is a very E-Z crowd pleaser and works for breakfast, lunch, or a snack. Open the french bread tube. Leaving the loaf round, cut half-inch pieces so that you have what looks like an ordinary biscuit. (By the way, biscuits will work, but do not taste the same and aren't as good as the french loaf). Place a sausage in each one of the pieces of french loaf and fold over, mashing the edges so that it does not come open. (Now it looks like a kolache, which is what we are after.)

Cooking method: Bake @ 400 degrees. Place piglets on cookie sheet and place in the oven. Bake 15 to 20 minutes or until golden brown. Enjoy.

HINT: This recipe came from Gibbs and Jan Goodwin, probably two of the nicest people I have ever met in my life, out of all the places I have visited. Just plain down-to-earth. So take ten minutes and make some Crazy Crackers. You will love them, I promise.

TIP: If you are up to a challenge and ever in or going through Ellisville, Mississippi off Interstate 59, I would suggest calling ahead, 601-477-4800, and making reservations to spend a day on the ropes course at Challenge Country, owned, operated, and designed by Gibbs and Jan Goodwin. You will create an unbelievable bond of trust between you, your family, friends, or co-workers. GO CHECK IT OUT!

CRAZY CRACKERS

INGREDIENTS
4 sleeves saltine crackers
1 cup canola oil
1 pkg. ranch dressing mix
1/2 tsp. red pepper
1 tsp. red pepper seeds

TOOLS
large one gal. container w/ top
small bowl or jar
whisk or spoon

Pre-prep: Put crackers in large one gal. container. Mix together oil, ranch dressing, red pepper, and red pepper seeds in small bowl. Blend well. Pour over crackers, cover, and gently roll until all crackers are covered, 1 minute or so and repeat this 4 or 5 times. Put in zipper-style bag.

Note: You might want to make two batches. The first batch will probably be gone before you ever leave for your outing.

FAVORITE RECIPES

NAME OF RECIPE	PAGE

35

HINT: This salad is a pretty much an all-around salad and will go with just about any meal.

TIP: If you don't want to mess with this at camp, go ahead and pre-prep them and place in individual zipper-style bags. When at camp, eat straight from the bag.

SPINACH SALAD
(ONLY ONE E-Z WAY)

INGREDIENTS
1 bag spinach leaves
  (pre-washed/cleaned)
1 jar Marie's spinach dressing
parmesan cheese (optional to taste)

TOOLS
paper bowls
spork/fork

Camp-prep: When shopping for your menu, pick up the pre-washed/ cleaned spinach in a bag. Leave it in the bag and refrigerate or ice until ready to make. Put about 25 to 30 leaves in a bowl and spoon 3 tbsp. of dressing onto spinach and serve. (You could have figured this out for yourself, huh?) Enjoy.

HINT: I know this one sounds a little (okay a lot) stupid, but I am serious, it is the cheapest way to get by on this one.

TIP: If you do go out and buy all the fruit and make it from scratch, you will need to increase you pre-prep window by about 45 minutes (just trying to make it easy on you).

FRUIT SALAD

OFF-ROAD, CAMPING & RV'ERS STYLE

INGREDIENTS
1 medium fruit platter

TOOLS
zipper bag large

Pre-prep: Start by taking the fruit platter and dumping it in a large zipper-style bag, ice or refrigerate until ready to serve. This is by far the most economical way to have fruit salad.

HINT: If you're like me and can't just have soup for dinner, plan two recipes for this meal. One that goes really well with the soup is the Oysters Rockefeller and crackers.

TIP: When combining the soup with another recipe, I recommend waiting until the soup is almost ready before cooking the second item, so that your second item will not get cold; plus, it will not hurt a thing for the soup to simmer an extra twenty or thirty minutes.

VEGGIE-HEAD SOUP

OFF-ROAD & CAMPING STYLE

INGREDIENTS
1 green bell pepper
1 red bell pepper
1/2 c. sweet onions
4 green onions
  (cut into pieces)
1 zucchini (diced)
1/2 c. green beans
  (canned or frozen)
2/3 c. sliced carrots

2 - 14.5 oz. cans veg-
  etable or chicken broth
1 - 14.5-oz. can diced
  tomatoes (with juice)
2 tbsp. olive oil
2 tsp. minced garlic
4 pinches pepper
2 pinches salt
1 pinch basil
1 pinch oregano

TOOLS
knife
large spoon
paper bowls
dutch oven
charcoal
charcoal starter

Pre-prep: Dice, cut, chop all ingredients, and put in one zipper-style bag. Then measure all the spices and put them into a bag. Take the canned and other ingredients and put them all into one large zipper-style bag. (When buying your cans, try to get them with the pop-open lids; it will save time and tools).

Cooking method: Dutch oven. Use 2/3 the briquettes on the bottom and 1/3 the briquettes on the lid. Add oil. Sauté' the veggies (except the zucchini; this will be added the last 20 minutes). Once veggies are transparent, then add the tomatoes and broth. Simmer for 20 minutes, rotating the oven every 10 minutes. Add spices and zucchini, stir, and continue simmering for another 20 minutes, still rotating the oven. Serve hot.

RV'ERS STYLE

TOOLS
knife
large spoon
soup pot
stove top

Per-prep or Camp-prep: Dice, cut, chop all ingredients, and put in one zipper-style bag or straight into a hot soup pot (4 qt.). Then measure all the spices and put them into a bag or into the pot. (When buying your cans, try to get them with the pop-open lids; it will save time and tools).

Cooking method: Stovetop, high heat. Add oil. Sauté' the veggies (except the zucchini; this will be added in the last 20 minutes). Once veggies are transparent, then add the tomatoes and broth. Simmer for 20 minutes uncovered, then add spices and zucchini; stir and continue simmering for another 20 minutes. Serve hot.

HINT: For the vegetarians out there, this is a good one for you guys to replace the beef with green peppers, squash, zucchini, beans, etc. See the tip for cooking method.

TIP: When using veggies, you will want to sauté the veggies in 1 tbsp. garlic and 2 tbsp. butter. Place in zipper-style bag. This will cut down on camp-prep and will insure that they will not be uncooked or raw. Okay, got to add this in: My buddy Terry Estes likes to take the leftovers from the chili and add Frito-style chips and cheddar cheese to use for lunch the next day. See Frito Pie Burritos in the Manifold Lunch Section.

ALMOST MAMA'S CHILI (ONLY QUICKER)

OFF-ROAD & CAMPING STYLE

INGREDIENTS
1 can Chili Magic (spicy style)
1 lb. ground beef
1 large chopped onion
1 tbsp. minced garlic
1 can Ro-Tel tomatoes
2 - 14.5 oz. cans diced tomatoes

TOOLS
dutch oven
large spoon
charcoal
starter fluid
hot mitts

Camp-prep: Dutch oven. Use all the coals on the bottom with the lid on for 5 minutes. Start by browning the ground beef, onions, and garlic. Once browned, drain grease and add the remaining ingredients. Remove half of the briquettes from the bottom and put on the lid and simmer for 30 minutes. Serve with crackers.

RV'ERS STYLE

TOOLS
soup pot
large spoon
stovetop
hot pad holder

Camp-prep: Start by browning the ground beef, onions, and garlic. Once browned, drain grease and add the remaining ingredients.

Cooking method: Stovetop on medium. Simmer for 30 minutes. Serve with crackers.

43

HINT: This is a very lengthy recipe for the campers and off-roaders, I would recommend waiting on this one until you have conquered the dutch oven and feel good about it. For all of you with plenty of experience, I would say go for it. This is a very tasty dish.

TIP: The quickest way to heat up this recipe is probably to use freezer-style zipper bags (instead of mason jars) and heat in boiling water for 15-20 minutes. This way, there is no glass in the camp area for the little ones to get hurt or cut, if someone happens to drop or break their mason jar, nor will the persons using the same campsite after you have gone home.

CLAM CHOWDER

OFF-ROAD & CAMPING STYLE

INGREDIENTS

TOOLS

1 doz. fresh cherrystone clams
   (canned clams will do)
1 c. water
5 slices bacon
1 tbsp. butter
1 large onion, diced (about 2 cups)
2 tbsp. all-purpose flour
6 potatoes cut into 1/2" pieces
   (about 2 cups)
1 1/2 tsp. dried thyme
2 pinches pepper, or to taste
1 c. milk
1 c. heavy cream (whipping)
3 tbsp. parsley

camp stove
large spoon
knife
mason jars (1 pint)
dutch oven
charcoal
charcoal starter

Pre-prep: Place fresh clams in large soup pot with water. Cover and cook over medium heat until clams open. Remove and set aside. Throw any unopened clams in trash. Take clams out of shell and chop well. Save the stock to use later. Cook the bacon in the pot so that fat is rendered and edges are brown (about 5 minutes). Add butter and onions. Cook until onions are wilted (10 minutes), then add flour and cook another 5 minutes. Add the stock that you set aside from the clams, potatoes, thyme, and pepper. Simmer 5 minutes; now add the clams and cook 12 minutes or until tender; do not overcook. The final step is to add the milk and cream, stirring well over LOW heat. Do not boil, this will cause it to curdle. Adjust the seasoning and add parsley. Store in one-pint mason jars with lids.

Cooking method: Dutch oven. Fill Dutch oven half full of water. Put all briquettes underneath oven. Place mason jars in water and reheat for 30 to 40 minutes or until hot. (Loosen seal on jars so that the pressure will escape when heating.)

HINT: RV'ers unless your camped over looking the Chesapeck Bay waching the sail boats sail by you are going to be hard pressed to find fresh clams. I would recommend using canned clams, as fresh clams are not available year around.

TIP: The quickest way to heat up this recipe, if pre-preped, is probably to use freezer-style zipper bags (instead of mason jars) and heat in boiling water for 15-20 minutes. This way, there is no glass in the camp area for the little ones to get hurt or cut, if someone happens to drop or break their mason jar, nor will the persons using the same campsite after you have gone home.

CLAM CHOWDER

INGREDIENTS

1 doz. fresh cherrystone clams
  (canned clams will do)
1 c. water
5 slices bacon
1 tbsp. butter
1 large onion, diced (about 2 cups)
2 tbsp. all-purpose flour
6 potatoes cut into 1/2" pieces
  (about 2 cups)
1 1/2 tsp. dried thyme
2 pinches pepper, or to taste
1 c. milk
1 c. heavy cream (whipping)
3 tbsp. parsley

TOOLS

soup pot
measuring cup
large spoon
stovetop

Pre-prep or Camp-prep: Place fresh clams in large soup pot with water. Cover and cook over medium heat until clams open. Remove and set aside. Throw any unopened clams in trash. Take clams out of shell and chop well. Save the stock to use later. Cook the bacon in the pot so that fat is rendered and edges are brown (about 5 minutes). Add butter and onions. Cook until onions are wilted (10 minutes), then add flour and cook another 5 minutes. Add the stock that you set aside from the clams, potatoes, thyme, and pepper. Simmer 5 minutes. Now add the clams and cook 12 minutes or until tender; do not overcook. Final step is to add the milk and cream, stirring well over LOW heat. Do not boil, this will cause it to curdle. Adjust the seasoning and add parsley. Store in large, airtight container.

Cooking method: Micro or stovetop heat (only what you need) over medium heat until piping hot. Serve in nice bowl with clam crackers.

HINT: Let's take this one a little further. Prepare the gumbo completely at home and store in freezer-style bags. When at camp, boil water in a soup pot and use the boiling water to heat and then eat, straight from the bag. 15-20 minutes.

TIP: I could not stop myself from this one. When using road kill, the best way to insure that it is fresh, on your way to work the day before your outing, you will need to take some fluorescent paint with you and paint a circle around all the road kill between your house and work. When finished with work on your way home, everything without a circle around it would be considered fresh.

REDNECK (ANYTHING GOES) GUMBO
(REMEMBER THIS IS "ANYTHING GOES." SUBSTITUTE WITH VENISON, BEAR, LOBSTER, CRAB, ROAD KILL, ETC...)

OFF- ROAD & CAMPING STYLE

INGREDIENTS
4 oz. Lil Smokies (cut 1/2" dice)
2 tbsp. olive oil
1 - 14-oz. can okra
1 c. onions (diced)
1/2 c. green bell peppers (minced)
1/2 c. red bell peppers (minced)
2 cloves garlic (minced)
2 - 14.5-oz. cans chicken broth
1 - 24-oz. can diced tomatoes
1/2 tsp. ground cumin
2 pinches salt
2 pinches pepper
1 bay leaf
1/2 pound shrimp (25 to 40 count)
1/2 pound your choice (scallops,
   chicken, road kill, etc.)
1/8 pound lump crabmeat

TOOLS
knife
large spoon
dutch oven
charcoal
charcoal starter
hot mitts
tongs

Per-prep: Start by cutting, chopping, and dicing all of your veggies and meats. Once complete, store them in zipper bags, onions in one, peppers in one, spices in one, and so on. Group and label.

Cooking method: Dutch oven. Use all the briquettes underneath. Sauté the Lil' Smokies 5 minutes, then add the oil and sauté the veggies along with the spices, 10 minutes, then add the tomatoes and broth. Take 1/3 of your briquettes from the bottom and place them on the lid. Simmer for 25 minutes and then add the anything-goes part, shrimp, scallops, and lobster. Cook an additional 10 minutes; serve hot.

Note: If you are using chicken, bear, road kill, these items should be added along with the tomatoes and broth.

HINT: This is a good one to cook when your on a trip with your RVing buddies. They will love you for miles and miles

TIP: I could not stop myself from this one. When using road kill, the best way to insure that it is fresh, on your way to work the day before your outing, you will need to take some fluorescent paint with you and paint a circle around all the road kill between your house and work. When finished with work on your way home, everything without a circle around it would be considered fresh.

REDNECK (ANYTHING GOES) GUMBO
(REMEMBER, ANYTHING GOES. SUBSTITUTE CAVIAR, LOBSTER, POMPANO, SOLE, SCALLOPS, ETC...)

RV'ERS STYLE

INGREDIENTS
4 oz. Lil Smokies (cut 1/2" dice)
2 tbsp. olive oil
1 - 14-oz. can okra
1 c. onions (diced)
1/2 c. green bell peppers (minced)
1/2 c. red bell peppers (minced)
2 cloves garlic (minced)
2 - 14.5-oz. cans chicken broth
1 - 24-oz. can diced tomatoes
1/2 tsp. ground cumin
2 pinches salt
2 pinches pepper
1 bay leaf
1/2 pound shrimp (25 to 40 count)
1/2 pound your choice (scallops,
   chicken, road kill, etc.)
1/8 pound lump crabmeat

TOOLS
soup pot
knife
large spoon
stovetop high heat

Camp-prep: Start by cutting, chopping, and dicing all of your veggies and meats; set aside.

Cooking method: Stovetop on high heat. first sauté the Lil' Smokies, then add oil and sauté the veggies and spices about 10 minutes in all. Add tomatoes and broth and simmer over medium heat for 25 minutes. Add seafood and simmer another 10 minutes; serve hot.

51

HINT: When finished eating dinner, if there are any leftovers, don't throw them away. Store them in zipper-style bags and ice or refrigerate. Better yet, if you still have any energy, go ahead and make burritos with the meat and veggies for the next day's lunch and wrap individually. (See Manifold Lunches.)

TIP: Try using the RV'ers cooking methods if there is only one dutch oven present, and use the dutch oven for Garlic and Cheese Biscuits (see Biscuits in Breakfast Section). RV'ers, you have got to try these biscuits in the dutch oven. (Follow Off-Road and Camping Style.)

NO-PEEK STEW

OFF-ROAD & CAMPING STYLE

INGREDIENTS
1 lb. lean stew meat (1/2" dice)
1 tbsp. oil
1 small onion, chopped
1 1/2 cups thinly sliced carrots
1 cup thinly sliced celery
1 cup sliced mushrooms
1 - 32-oz. pkg. frozen southern-style
  hash-brown potatoes
1 envelope dry beef-mushroom
  soup mix
1/4 tsp. dried thyme leaves, crushed
1/4 tsp. pepper
3 1/2 c. water

TOOLS
dutch oven
large spoon
charcoal
charcoal starter

Pre-prep: Cut or buy pre-cut meat and place in zipper-style bag. Measure thyme and pepper and put in bag with meat. Chop onion, slice carrots, celery, and mushrooms. Place together in another zipper-style bag. Group and label. Store in fridge or ice until ready to cook.

Cooking method: Dutch oven. Use 2/3 of the briquettes on the bottom and 1/3 on the lid. Add oil and sauté beef until brown. Add veggies and cook for 5 minutes. Add water and soup mix; mix well. Cover and simmer for 30 minutes. Remember, NO PEEKING! Serve hot with crackers or biscuits.

RV'ERS STYLE

TOOLS
stovetop or crock pot
soup pot
large spoon

Pre-prep or Camp-prep: For pre-prep, follow instructions above. For camp-prep, start by cutting stew meat into 1/2" dice. Then cut, slice, and chop veggies.

Cooking method: Stovetop over medium-high heat. Heat soup pot on high until hot. Add oil. Add meat and brown. Reduce to medium high. Add veggies and cook for 2 minutes. Add remaining ingredients, cover, and simmer for 20 minutes. Serve hot.

Approximate Chicken Cooking Times				
Type of Chicken	Weight	Roasting 350 °F	Simmering	Grilling
Whole broiler fryer+	3 to 4 lbs.	1 1/4 - 1 1/2 hrs.	60 to 75 min.	60 to 75 min*
Whole roasting hen+	5 to 7 lbs.	2 to 2 1/4 hrs.	1 3/4 to 2 hrs.	18 - 25 min./lb*
Whole capon+	4 to 8 lbs.	2 to 3 hrs	Not suitable	15 - 20 min/lb*
Whole Cornish hens+	18 - 24 oz.	50 to 60 min.	35 to 40 min.	45 to 55 min*
Breast halves, bone-in	6 - 8 oz.	30 to 40 min.	35 to 45 min.	10 - 15 min./side
Breast half, boneless	4 ounces	20 to 30 min.	25 to 30 min.	6 - 8 min./side
Legs or thighs	8 or 4 oz.	40 to 50 min.	40 to 50 min.	10 - 15 min./side
Drumsticks	4 ounces	35 to 45 min.	40 to 50 min.	8 to 12 min./side
Wings or wingettes	2 to 3 oz.	30 to 40 min.	35 to 45 min.	8 to 12 min./side

+ Unstuffed. If stuffed, add 15 to 30 minutes additional time.
* Indirect method using drip pan.

55

HINT: This is a good one to cook if there are a lot of people in your group. Unlike the french bread piglets, this dish will go a long way as far as getting everyone filled up and making them happy. Enjoy.

TIP: When using the zipper-style bags for storing items such as sour cream, gravies, sauces and so on. When ready to start using these ingredients, cut one of the corners off of the bottom of the bag. These ingredients are better squeezed out through the cut corner than trying to spoon them out the same way you spooned them in.

CBC WITH RICE
(CHICKEN BROCCOLI CHEESE)

INGREDIENTS
4 boneless, skinless chicken breasts
1 bag boil-in-bag rice (white)
1 can cream of mushroom soup
1 can cheddar cheese soup
1 cup sour cream
2 cups fresh broccoli (1 large crown)
1 tsp. pepper
1/2 tsp. salt (to taste)

TOOLS
large spoon
dutch oven
charcoal
starter fluid
knife

Pre-prep: Cut chicken to a 1" dice, and place in small zipper style bag. Cut stems off broccoli (use tops) place in zipper _____ (fill in blank) bag. Measure sour cream and place in zipper-style _____ (fill in blank). Boil rice and you got it, put it in a zipper-style bag. Place all bags in one large zipper-style bag along with the two cans of soup and label.

Cooking method: Dutch oven. Use 1/3 briquettes on bottom and 2/3 briquettes on top. Place all ingredients (except rice) in dutch oven and stir. Cook 40-50 minutes. Remember to rotate oven every 15 minutes. The last 15 minutes, add rice, and do not stir. Serve hot.

RV'ERS STYLE

TOOLS
oven @ 350 degrees
casserole dish (9x9 or so)
hot pad holders
sauce pan
Football game on dish satellite

Camp-prep: Cut chicken to a 1" dice. Cut broccoli (use tops). Measure sour cream. Open cans. Place all ingredients (except rice) in casserole dish and stir well.

Cooking method: Oven @ 350 degrees for 50 minutes. Cook rice per packet instructions. Serve hot over rice.

HINT: Okay, there maybe a little extra clean up on this recipe, because this one warrants real plates, not paper.

TIP: You may need a veggie to go with this one; one that goes great is fresh broccoli. The last 15 minutes of cooking time, add the broccoli (pre-cut during pre-prep to bite-size pieces) on top of the chicken and finish cooking. (See dutch oven cooking tips.)

CHICKEN CORDON BLEU W/ROASTED POTATOES

OFF-ROAD & CAMPING STYLE

INGREDIENTS

		TOOLS
4 boneless, skinless chicken breasts	1 egg, beaten	dutch oven
2 tsp. Dijon mustard	1/3 cup corn flake crumbs	plastic wrap
4 tsp. chopped fresh chives	4 medium potatoes	toothpicks
4 thin slices cooked lean ham	1 tsp. garlic powder	hot mitts
4 slices swiss cheese	1 tbsp. parsley	metal tongs
	1 tbsp. oil	charcoal
		charcoal starter

Pre-prep: Start by placing 1 chicken breast in plastic wrap and pound flat so that chicken breast is about 1/4" thick. Repeat with remaining breasts. Place 1/2 tsp. of mustard on each breast, along with 1 tsp. of chives for each. Put ham and cheese on and cut to fit. Roll up, making sure that ends are tucked in. Toothpick together and place in zipper-style bag. Cut potatoes to 3/4" dice and place in zipper-style bag and cover potatoes with water (to prevent browning). Put corn flakes in zipper-style bag. Combine garlic and parsley into one bag. Group, label, and refrigerate.

Cooking method: Dutch oven. Use 1/2 briquettes on the bottom and 1/2 briquettes on the lid. Drain and dry potatoes. Add oil and potatoes. Sprinkle garlic powder and parsley mixture over top of potatoes. Place beaten egg in bag with chicken, making sure that each breast is coated well. Then take breasts one at a time and place in bag with corn flakes. Coat well. Once coated, place breasts on top of potatoes. Cook 45 minutes, rotating oven every 15 minutes.

RV'ERS STYLE

TOOLS
oven @ 400 degrees
8-inch square (2-quart) baking dish
nonstick spray
hot pad holders
cookie sheet
spatula

Pre-prep: For pre-prep, follow the instructions above.

Cooking method: Oven @ 400 degrees. Spray baking dish and cookie sheet with nonstick spray. Drain and dry potatoes. Place potatoes on cookie sheet and sprinkle garlic powder and parsley mixture over top of potatoes. Place potatoes in oven for 45 minutes. Dip each breast in beaten egg until breast is coated well. Place breast in bag with corn flakes. Coat well. Once coated, place breasts in baking dish. Bake 35 minutes. 59

HINT: You have probably noticed that one of the veggies of choice is broccoli. That is because broccoli stores well and can be prepared very easily and in many different ways with a variety of different recipes.

TIP: When shopping for items to prepare, the ones that call for garlic, instead of getting it in the cloves, look for the minced garlic in a jar in the veggie section. This will knock at least 5 minutes off of your prep time per meal (4 meals, that's 20 minutes). There is very little if any difference in taste.

ROASTED CHICKEN
W/POTATOES, CARROTS, & BROCCOLI

OFF-ROAD & CAMPING STYLE

INGREDIENTS
whole chicken, cut up
1 1/2 cups potatoes, 1/2" dice
1 1/2 cups carrots, thinly sliced
2 cups broccoli
1 tbsp. water
1/2 tsp. salt
1/2 tsp. pepper
1 tsp. Adobe or Lawry's seasoning
1 tbsp fresh garlic

TOOLS
dutch oven
charcoal
knife
hot mitts
charcoal starter
large spoon

Pre-prep: Cut chicken or buy pre-cut. Place in zipper-style bag. Cut potatoes. Place in zipper-style bag and cover with water (to prevent browning). Cut carrots and broccoli. Place together in zipper-style bag. Combine salt, pepper, and seasoning in one zipper-style bag. Group and label.

Cooking method: Dutch oven. Use 1/2 briquettes on the bottom and 1/2 briquettes on lid. Place chicken in bottom of oven, along with water. Using half of seasoning mixture, sprinkle over chicken. Drain potatoes. Place all veggies on top of chicken. Sprinkle with remaining seasoning mixture. Cook 50 minutes, rotating every 15 minutes. (See dutch oven cooking tips.)

RV'ERS STYLE

TOOLS
oven @ 425 degrees
9x13 baking dish
hot pad holders
foil

Pre-prep: Cut chicken or buy pre-cut. Place in zipper-style bag. Cut potatoes. Place in zipper-style bag and cover with water (to prevent browning). Cut carrots and broccoli. Place together in zipper-style bag. Combine salt, pepper, and seasoning in one zipper-style bag. Group and label.

Cooking method: Oven @ 425 degrees. Place chicken in bottom of baking dish along with water. Using half of seasoning mixture, sprinkle over chicken. Drain potatoes. Place all veggies on top of chicken. Sprinkle with remaining seasoning mixture. Cover with foil and cook for 35 minutes. Remove foil, drain fat, and cook uncovered for another 15 minutes or until juices from chicken are clear. Serve hot.

HINT: RV'ers, this one is very tasty in the oven on broil, but please try this one on the grill at least once. You will not be disappointed.

TIP: As far as the Italian dressing goes, I buy the cheap stuff ($0.99). I have tried just about every brand out there, and the end result is the same. Now, the homemade Italian dressing from family or friends, well, there is no substitution for the best.

ITALIAN GRILLED CHICKEN

OFF-ROAD, CAMPING & RV'ERS STYLE

INGREDIENTS
4 chicken breasts w/ribs
16 oz. Italian dressing (cheap)
1 green bell pepper
1 red bell pepper
1 onion (sweet)
1/2 lb. whole mushrooms
1 zucchini
1 boil-in-bag rice

TOOLS
grill
charcoal
tongs
wooden skewers
knife
charcoal starter

Pre-prep: Wash and place chicken in large zipper bag with half of the Italian dressing. Cut peppers, onions, and zucchini into 1-inch pieces. On skewers, place green pepper, red pepper, onion, green pepper, red pepper; okay, I know, you get the picture. Once complete, place one mushroom on each end of all skewers (to prevent puncture of bag) Place skewers in bag, along with other half of dressing. Group, label, and refrigerate. This recipe is not rocket science, but it sure is good.

Cooking method: Grill (20 to 25 briquettes). When your coals are ready, remove chicken and veggies from the bags and get 'em on the grill. The veggie skewers you will want to rotate frequently (every 2 minutes or so). The chicken will take 15 to 20 minutes to cook, turning just once. Serve hot.

HINT: You may use any type of game bird — quail, dove, grouse, pigeon, etc. The reason I have used Cornish game hens is that they are available year-round at your local supermarket.

TIP: Try using a slice of jalapeño. Place it in the cavity of the bird (no seeds, unless you want it HOT and then you're on your own) and then wrap the entire out side with bacon and use toothpicks to secure. Then follow cooking methods.

CORNISH GAME HENS W/ POTATOES)

OFF-ROAD & CAMPING STYLE

INGREDIENTS
4 Cornish game hens
4 medium red potatoes
3 tbsp. butter
1 tbsp. garlic
1 tsp. black pepper
1/2 tsp. salt
4 ears corn (on camp stove)

TOOLS
large fork
dutch oven
charcoal
hot mitts
camp stove
soup pot (for corn)
charcoal starter

Pre-prep: Hens are more than likely packaged individually. Cut potatoes so that when you finish, you have round slices about 1/4" thick; place in zipper bag and cover with water (to prevent browning). Place garlic powder, pepper, and salt in a zipper _____(fill in blank) bag. Group and label.

Cooking method: Dutch oven. Use 2/3 briquettes on bottom and 1/3 briquettes on the lid. Melt butter. Layer potatoes on bottom. After you have finished that, place the game hen on top of the potatoes. Grab the spice bag and sprinkle over hens and potatoes. Cook 40 minutes, rotating oven every 15 minutes (See dutch oven cooking tips.)

RV'ERS STYLE

TOOLS
oven @ 350 degrees
casserole dish
soup pot (for corn)
knife
large fork
foil

Pre-prep or Camp-prep: Hens are more than likely packaged individually. Cut potatoes so that when you finish, you have round slices about 1/4" thick. Place in zipper bag and cover with water (to prevent browning). Place garlic powder, pepper, and salt in a zipper bag. Place all ingredients in large zipper bag, label, and store.

Cooking method: Oven @ 350 degrees. Melt butter in casserole dish. Layer potatoes on bottom. After you have finished that, place the game hen on top of the potatoes. Grab the spice bag and sprinkle over hens and potatoes. Cover with foil and cook 40 minutes.

HINT: You may use any type of game bird, Cornish game hens, dove, grouse, pigeon, etc... Cornish game hens are available year-round at your local supermarket.

TIP: Spice it up a little and make the White Cajun Sauce in the Side Dish Section. 2 tbsp. over each bird just before serving. Not a bad combo.

GRILL ROASTED QUAIL

OFF-ROAD & CAMPING STYLE

INGREDIENTS
8 breast of quail (deboned)
4 jalapenos (cut in half)
8 large shrimp (shelled)
8 strips bacon
1/8 tsp. salt
1/8 tsp. pepper
1/8 tsp. adobo seasoning

TOOLS
grill/grate/ campfire
charcoal
charcoal starter
toothpicks
knife
favorite beverage

Pre-prep: Start by deboning quail breast. Cut jalapenos in half lengthways. Shell and de-vein shrimp, then butterfly. Lay quail breast flat and place the half jalapeno on breast, then shrimp on that, sprinkle salt, pepper, and adobo seasoning on breast of quail and over pepper and shrimp, roll breast jelly roll style so that it is tight. Then wrap with bacon and secure with toothpick. Group, label, and refrigerate.

Cooking method: Grill. Start by lighting grill. Once coals are ready (gray) place grate over coals to heat. Place stuffed quail breast on grate, cooking 5 minutes, turning every 5 minutes until bacon is fully cooked, about 25 minutes. Serve with veggie.

RV'ERS STYLE

TOOLS
oven @ broil 450 degrees
broiling pan
toothpicks
knife
favorite beverage

Pre-prep or Camp-prep: Start by deboning quail breast. Cut jalapenos in half lengthways. Shell and de-vein shrimp, then butterfly. Lay quail breast flat and place the half jalapeno on breast, then shrimp on that, sprinkle salt, pepper, and adobo seasoning on breast of quail and over pepper and shrimp, roll breast jelly roll style so that it is tight. Then wrap with bacon and secure with toothpick.

Cooking methods: Broil 450 degrees. Place quail breast on broiler pan, and throw in the oven. Broil for 20 to 25 minutes, turning every 5 minutes until bacon is done and crisp. Serve hot with your favorite veggie.

HINT: When starting the charcoal in the grill, add the number of briquettes you need to cook dessert in the dutch oven, Pineapple Upside-Down Cake. An excellent meal deserves a tasty dessert.

TIP: This recipe with a side of rice and refried beans cooked on the stove at camp is probably the best way to complement this meal.

CHICKEN MONTEREY
(ONLY ONE WAY OF THIS ONE)

OFF-ROAD, CAMPING, & RV'ERS STYLE

INGREDIENTS
4 boneless skinless breasts (chicken)
8 slices bacon, cooked
1/2 cup bbq sauce (your choice)
4 slices monterey jack cheese
1 small tomato, sliced thin
1 avocado, sliced
salt and pepper to taste
1 can refried beans
prepared spanish rice (per cooked
  boil-in-bag)

TOOLS
grill
charcoal
spatula
foil
spoon
charcoal starter

Camp-prep: Put beans on foil (large amount of foil to make air pocket on top). Fold foil over and seal on sides and top. Place Spanish rice in separate foil and seal. Place on grill while chicken is grilling.

Cooking method: Grill chicken until done, 15-20 minutes. Place 2 tbsp. BBQ sauce on each breast. Top with bacon, tomato, and cheese. Grill for 5 minutes. Remove and add avocado on top. Serve with refried beans and Spanish rice.

69

Approximate Beef Cooking Times °F				
Type of Beef	Size	Cooking Method	Cooking Time	Internal Temperature
Rib Roast, bone in	4 to 6 lbs.	Roast 325°	23-25 min./lb.	Medium rare 145°
Rib Roast, boneless rolled	4 to 6 lbs.	Roast 325°	Add 5-8 min./lb. to time above	Medium rare 145°
Chuck Roast, Brisket	3 to 4 lbs.	*Braise 325°	45-50 min./lb.	Medium 160°
Round or Rump Roast	2 1/2 to 4 lbs.	Roast 325°	30-35 min./lb.	Medium rare 145°
Tenderloin, whole	4 to 6 lbs.	Roast 425°	45-60 min. total.	Medium rare 145°
Steaks	3/4" thick	Broil/Grill	4-5 min. per side	Medium rare 145°
Stew or Shank Cross Cuts	1 to 1 1/2" thick	Cover with liquid; simmer	2 to 3 hours	Medium 160°
Short Ribs	4" long and 2" thick	*Braise 325°	1 1/2 to 2 1/2 hours	Medium 160°

* Indirect method using drip pan.

71

HINT: For the RV'ers, for this recipe can be camp-prepped, but will be more fun and less work if this recipe is pre-prepped before you leave for your outing.

TIP: Please when purchasing your zipper-style bags, don't buy the cheapest generic bags. Your best bet on this is to go with the name-brand bags when using liquids, as generics don't work well.

DRESSED-UP CUBE STEAKS

OFF-ROAD & CAMPING STYLE

INGREDIENTS
4 beef cubed steaks (6 oz. each)
1 clove garlic, minced
1 tbsp. vegetable oil
1 cup prepared stuffing
1/4 cup grated parmesan cheese
1 cup water
3/4 cup chili sauce
1 tsp. beef bouillon or cube

TOOLS
dutch oven
charcoal
knife
hot mitts
toothpicks
charcoal starter

Pre-prep: Prepare stuffing according to box. Let cool. Sauté peppers, onion, and garlic in oil until tender-crisp; remove. Place in zipper-style bag. In small bowl, combine stuffing and parmesan cheese. Place 1/4 cup stuffing mixture on each steak. Roll, jelly-roll fashion, and secure with toothpicks. Brown steaks and let cool. Place in zipper-style bag. Combine salt, pepper, and seasoning in one zipper-style bag. Put water, chili sauce, and beef bouillon in one zipper-style bag. Group and label.

Cooking method: Dutch oven. Use 2/3 briquettes on the bottom and 1/3 briquettes on lid. Place steak rolls in bottom of oven. If using veggies, pour bag with veggies over steaks and then pour sauce over everything. Cook 40 minutes, rotating every 15 minutes. (See dutch oven cooking tips)

RV'ERS STYLE

TOOLS
knife
large skillet
saucepan
stove top (med. high)
toothpicks

Pre-prep or Camp-prep: Stove top. Prepare stuffing per box and set aside. In small bowl, mix stuffing and parmesan cheese. Put 1/4 cup stuffing mixture on each steak and roll like a jelly roll; use toothpicks to secure. In a large skillet, brown steaks using a little oil if needed. Mix water, chili sauce, beef bouillon in bowl and if using veggies, place over steak rolls, then pour over everything.

Cooking method: Stovetop med. High heat. Cover and let simmer 30 minutes, basting steaks every 15 minutes. Serve by spooning sauce over rolls. Enjoy!

HINT: About the easiest Mexican dish you will find anywhere. You can prepare this one at home following the RV'ers Style in a casserole dish or if you have a crock pot, and there is still little to no maintenance.

TIP: Okay, for this one, if you want, you can replace the ground beef with steak, chicken, venison, veggies, or whatever else you can come up with. The substitutes that I listed I have tried and work very well.

BEEF ENCHILADAS

OFF-ROAD & CAMPING STYLE

INGREDIENTS
1 pound ground beef
1 onion, chopped
1 can cream of mushroom soup
1 large jar picante sauce
4 cups grated cheese
1 pkg. corn tortillas

TOOLS
knife
large spoon
hot mitts
dutch oven
charcoal
charcoal starter

Pre-prep: Brown ground beef and onions in skillet. Drain fat and let cool. Mix soup, picante sauce, beef, onions and 2 cups cheese in bowl. Place in zipper-style bag. Keep tortillas in original bag. Group and label.

Cooking method: Dutch oven. Use 1/3 briquettes on bottom and 2/3 briquettes on the lid. Cut or tear tortillas. Place layers in oven as follows: 1 cup soup/beef mixture, 1/3 of tortillas, 1 cup soup/beef mixture, 1/3 tortillas, 1 cup soup/beef mixture, remaining tortillas, remaining soup/beef mixture and then top with remaining cheese. Cook 1 hour rotating every 15 minutes.

RV'ERS STYLE

TOOLS
oven @ 350 degrees
knife
large skillet
medium bowl
large spoon
1-cup measuring cup or coffee cup
casserole dish
foil

Pre-prep or Camp-prep: Brown ground beef and onions in skillet. Drain fat and let cool. Mix soup, picante sauce, beef, onions, and 2 cups cheese in bowl. Cut tortillas in wedges. Group and label or start the layers.

Cooking method: Oven @ 350 degrees. Place layers in dish as follows: 1 cup soup/beef mixture, 1/3 of tortillas, 1 cup soup/beef mixture, 1/3 tortillas, 1 cup soup/beef mixture, remaining tortillas, remaining soup/beef mixture, and then top with remaining cheese. Cover with foil and bake for 45 minutes. Remove foil and bake for another 15 minutes. Let stand for 10 minutes before serving.

HINT: Lazy man spaghetti is a good one to use at home if you are tight on time during the week and are tired of eating frozen dinners (not really healthy). Make each member of your family a serving, and store in the freezer until ready and boil as you would at camp.

TIP: Keep in mind that I recommend using freezer-style zipper bags when using boiling water to heat your meal. These bags are a little bit thicker and there will be no chance the bag will become fragile when hot.

LAZY MAN SPAGHETTI
(HEAT-N-EAT)

INGREDIENTS
1 jar prepared spaghetti sauce,
  (we prefer Prego zesty mushroom)
1 lb. ground beef
1 small package spaghetti noodles

TOOLS
large soup pot
spoon
strainer or lid of pan
camp stove

Pre-prep: Brown ground beef, drain fat. Mix with sauce. Cook spaghetti according to package. Drain and mix with sauce. Divide into 4 sandwich-size freezer-style zipper bags. Group, label, and freeze until time of departure.

Cooking Method: Camp stove over high heat. In large soup pot, boil 12 c. water. Add bags and boil for 10-15 minutes (depending on how frozen bags still are). Eat straight out of bag or put on dish and eat, whatever you desire.

RV'ERS STYLE

TOOLS
large saucepan
medium skillet
spoon
strainer or lid of pan
stovetop

Camp-Prep: Not much prep to this one.

Cooking Method: Stove medium-high. Brown ground beef, drain fat, and mix in sauce. Heat. Prepare noodles in saucepan according to package. Serve hot with garlic and cheese biscuits and salad.

HINT: Campers and off-roaders, this is just one more that can be tried at home. It's very easy to prepare and is pretty much a crowd pleaser. Serve with mashed potatoes and gravy.

TIP: A good side that works well at camp with the meatloaf — With the extra space you have on each side of the loaf, put number 1 or 2 new potatoes cut into quarters, and use one side for that and the other side for something like green beans. Everything will take the same amount of time.

MEATLOAF THE RIGHT WAY

OFF-ROAD & CAMPING STYLE

INGREDIENTS
1 lb. extra lean ground beef
1/2 cup green pepper, diced
1/2 cup red pepper, diced
1/2 cup onion, diced
1 c. bread crumbs. (italian flavored)
2 eggs
1 tsp. pepper
1 tsp. Adobo seasoning
1/2 tsp. salt
1/4 c. ketchup
1 tbsp. oil

TOOLS
large mixing bowl
spatula
dutch oven
charcoal
hot mitts
charcoal starter

Pre-prep: In large mixing bowl, mix all ingredients (except ketchup and oil) together with clean hands. Put mixture in a large zipper-style bag and refrigerate until ready to cook.

Cooking method: Dutch oven. Use 1/3 briquettes on the bottom and 2/3 briquettes on lid. Add 1 tbsp. oil. Place formed loaf in oven. Make sure that there is space on both sides of the oven. Top with ketchup. Cook 30-40 minutes, rotating oven every 15 minutes until done.

RV'ERS STYLE

TOOLS
oven @ 400 degrees
9X13 casserole dish
large mixing bowl
spatula
knife

Camp-prep or Pre-prep: In large mixing bowl, mix all ingredients (except ketchup and oil) together with clean hands. Refrigerate until ready to cook.

Cooking method: Oven @ 400 degrees. In the casserole dish, form a loaf from one end to the other, leaving about 2" on each side of loaf open. Top with ketchup and cook 30-40 minutes. Enjoy.

79

HINT: You will need to tell the persons eating that when they finish, they will need to kiss the cook, because this one is out of this world.

TIP: You can prepare this one at home completely, and when at camp, heat and eat from dutch oven or in a large skillet.

BEEF STROGANOFF

OFF-ROAD & CAMPING STYLE

INGREDIENTS
1 1/4 pounds boneless beef rib steak
2 tbsp. butter
1/4 cup onions (yellow sweet)
2 tbsp. minced garlic
1/2 tsp. pepper
1/2 tsp. salt
1 cup hot water
1 tbsp. all-purpose flour
1 tbsp. mustard
1 tbsp. tomato ketchup
2 cubes beef bouillon
3 tbsp. sour cream
1/2 package egg noodles

TOOLS
knife
large skillet
large spoon
camp stove
hot mitts

Pre-prep: Cut steak in 1" cubes; brown in skillet using 1 tbsp. butter. Remove from pan and let cool. Place in zipper-style bag. Sauté onion and garlic in remaining butter in same skillet (about 1 minute). Add mushrooms, salt and pepper (3 minutes), stirring occasionally. Set aside and cool. Place in zipper-style bag. Measure flour and put in separate zipper-style bag. Put water in zipper-style bag. Combine mustard, ketchup, and bouillon and put in another zipper-style bag. One more bag for sour cream and parsley. Cook egg noodles, add 1 tsp. oil to prevent noodles from sticking, let cool, and place in zipper-style bag. Group and label.

Cooking method: Camp stove. Medium/high — In a large skillet, heat the onion mixture. Sprinkle flour over onion mix and stir quickly for 2 minutes. Gradually add water. Water will start to thicken. Add mustard, ketchup, and bouillon. Stir. Add steak. Stir. Reduce heat, add sour cream. Stir in noodles. Cook until heated. Serve.

HINT: You will need to tell the persons eating that when they finish, they will need to kiss the cook, because this one is out of this world.

TIP: You can prepare this one at home completely, and when at camp, heat and eat from dutch oven or in a large skillet.

BEEF STROGANOFF

RV'ERS STYLE

INGREDIENTS
1 1/4 pounds boneless beef rib steak
2 tbsp. butter
1/4 cup onions (yellow sweet)
2 tbsp. minced garlic
1/2 tsp. pepper
1/2 tsp. salt
1 cup hot water
1 tbsp. all-purpose flour
1 tbsp. mustard
1 tbsp. tomato ketchup
2 cubes beef bouillon
3 tbsp. sour cream
1/2 package egg noodles

TOOLS
stovetop (medium-high heat)
knife
large skillet
medium saucepan
large spoon

Pre-prep: Cut steak in 1" cubes, brown in skillet using 1 tbsp. butter. Remove from pan and let cool. Place in zipper-style bag. Sauté onion and garlic in remaining butter in same skillet (about 1 minute); add mushrooms, salt, and pepper (3 minutes), stirring occasionally. Set aside and cool. Place in zipper-style bag. Measure flour and put in separate zipper-style bag. Put water in zipper-style bag. Combine mustard, ketchup, and bouillon and put in another zipper-style bag. Use one more bag for sour cream and parsley. Cook egg noodles, add 1 tsp. oil to prevent noodles from sticking, let cool, and place in zipper-style bag. Group and label.

Cooking method: Stovetop over medium-high heat. In a large skillet, heat the onion mixture. Sprinkle flour over onion mix and stir quickly (2 minutes). Gradually add water. Water will start to thicken. Add mustard, ketchup, and bouillon. Stir. Add steak. Stir. Reduce heat, add sour cream. Stir in noodles. Cook until heated and serve.

HINT: When the kebabs are finished, and it comes time to take them off the skewer, when you put them on, you use the sharp, pointed end. When you take them off, go the same way as when you put them on. (Slide them off the back off the skewer.)

TIP: If you like your beef medium-well to well-done, I would recommend putting the veggies on skewers by themselves. The beef will take a little while longer than the veggies.

TIP: Gotta have two tips for this one. If you would like to try something different when you put the kebabs in the zipper-style bag, dump some Italian dressing over them. When at camp, take them out of the bag and straight to the grill.

BEEF KEBABS
(DINNER ON A STICK)

INGREDIENTS
2 green peppers
2 red peppers
2 onions (medium)
1 - 8-oz. package mushrooms
1 1/2 lbs. steak (chuck eye round)
1/8 tsp. salt
1/8 tsp. pepper
1/8 tsp. Adobo

TOOLS
skewers
knife
charcoal
grill/grate/campfire
charcoal starter
tongs

Pre-prep: Start by cutting peppers and onions into 1 1/2" pieces and set aside. Do the same with the steak, 1 1/2" pieces. Now it's time to start the kebab part. Start with a mushroom; slide it down to the end. Then steak, green pepper, red pepper, onion, steak, green pepper, red pepper, onion, and so on. Once at the other end from where you started, place a mushroom at the end. Once all the skewers have been made, sprinkle your spices on the kebabs and place them in a zipper-style bag and refrigerate or ice until ready to cook.

Cooking method: Grill at about 350 degrees (20 to 25 briquettes). Once coals are ready, place the kebabs directly over coals. Turn quarter turn each time (every 3 minutes or so) and keep turning until done. For medium-temperature meat (warm pink center), this will take about 15 minutes. Enjoy!

HINT: For all the vegetarians out there, this is a good one for you guys to replace the beef with green peppers, squash, zucchini, beans, etc. The cook times will be the same.

TIP: When planning on this (lasagna) as being one of your meals for an outing, go ahead and plan to have a salad with this meal. Spinach salad is one that comes to mind.

SUPER SIMPLE BEEF LASAGNA

OFF-ROAD & CAMPING STYLE

INGREDIENTS

1 pound ground beef
2 - 10-oz. jars spaghetti sauce
1 3/4 cups (15-oz. container) ricotta
4 cups shredded mozzarella
1/2 cup grated parmesan cheese
2 eggs
1/4 cup chopped parsley
9 pieces lasagna noodles

TOOLS

knife
charcoal
large spoon
dutch oven
hot mitts
charcoal starter

Pre-prep: Brown ground beef in skillet. Drain fat. Add sauce to ground beef. Stir. Set aside to cool. Put in zipper-style bag. Mix ricotta, 1 cup of mozzarella, parmesan cheese with eggs and parsley. Place in zipper-style bag. Cook noodles 5 minutes. Put in another zipper-style bag. Group and label.

Cooking method: Dutch oven. Use 1/3 briquettes on the bottom 2/3 briquettes on the top. Place layers in oven as follows: 1 cup sauce, cover with one layer of noodles, 1 cup sauce, 1/2 cheese mixture, cover with one layer of noodles, 1 cup sauce, other half of cheese mixture, cover with one layer of noodles, remaining sauce and top with cheese.

RV'ERS STYLE

TOOLS
oven @ 350 degrees
large skillet
medium bowl
large spoon
9 x 13 baking dish
foil

Pre-prep: Brown ground beef in skillet. Drain fat. Add sauce to ground beef. Stir. Set aside to cool. Put in zipper-style bag. Mix ricotta, 1 cup of mozzarella, parmesan cheese with eggs and parsley. Place in zipper-style bag. Cook noodles for 5 minutes. Put in another zipper-style bag. Group and label.

Cooking method: Oven @ 350 degrees. Place layers in baking dish as follows: 1 cup sauce, cover with one layer of noodles, 1 cup sauce, 1/2 cheese mixture, cover with one layer of noodles, 1 cup sauce, other half of cheese mixture, cover with one layer of noodles, remaining sauce.and top with cheese. Cover with foill. Bake 45 minutes. Remove foil and bake another 15 minutes. Let stand 10 minutes before serving.

HINT: These "Elgin Hot Sausages" are unbelievable and are not so HOT like the name suggests. They may be purchased online at www.southsidemarket.com and are available cooked or uncooked. And well, if you're ever in Elgin, Texas, stop in and tell them that Grant Reid sent you. Personally, I prefer the uncooked, but they will take a little longer on the grill.

TIP: Southside Market & Barbeque™ "Elgin Hot Sausage" are a great and easy grilled dinner, and also make great leftovers for lunch the next day. Just wrap it in a tortilla with mustard or BBQ sauce. Enjoy.

"ELGIN HOT SAUSAGE"

INGREDIENTS
4 Southside Market & Barbeque™
  "Elgin Hot Sausages"
4 flour tortillas (or bread)
1 bottle of bbq sauce
1 jar mustard (some prefer over bbq
sauce)

TOOLS
grill/campfire/grate
charcoal
charcoal starter
tongs
cold beverage

Pre-prep: There is really no pre-prep on this one, but at least group this as a meal, and that's right, get out the zipper-style bags. "Elgin Hot Sausage" in one, tortillas or bread in one. Put both bags in one large bag with sauce and label.

Cooking method: Grill/campfire using 20-25 briquettes. Once you have good hot coals, arrange sausage around the coals so that they are not directly over the high heat and cook for 40 minutes, turning every 10 minutes. You will notice they will become brown and plump. Now move the sausage over the high heat, turning constantly so that they will not burn. This is so that the skin becomes tender. Once the skin pops, the juices will start to run out (watch the fire closely at this time). When that happens, it's time to eat. Set aside and use the coals to heat your tortillas.

Fresh Pork: Safe Cooking Chart

Internal temperature of safely cooked pork should reach 160 °F when measured with a meat thermometer.

ROAST: Set oven at 350 °F. Roast in a shallow pan, uncovered.
Internal temperature: 160° - medium; 170° - well done.

Type of Cut	Size	Cooking Method	Cooking Time
Loin Roast, Bone-in or Boneless	2 to 5 lbs.	Roast 350°	20-30 min./lb.
Crown Roast	4 - 6 lbs.	Roast 350°	20-30 min./lb.
Leg, (Fresh Ham) Whole, Bone-in	12 to 16 lbs.	Roast 350°	22-26 min./lb.
Leg, (Fresh Ham) Half, Bone-in	5 to 8 lbs.	Roast 350°	35-40 min./lb.
Boston Butt	3 - 6 lbs.	Roast 350°	45 min./lb.
Tenderloin	1/2 to 1 1/2 lbs.	Roast 425-450°	20 to 30 min. total
Ribs (Back, Country-style or Spareribs)	2 to 4 lbs.	Broil or Grill	1 1/2 to 2 hours (or until fork tender)
Loin Chops, Bone-in or Boneless	3/4" or 1 1/2"	Broil or Grill	6 - 8 minutes or 12 - 16 minutes
Tenderloin	1/2 to 1 1/2 lbs.	Broil or Grill	15 to 25 minutes
Ribs, all types	2 - 4 lbs.	Broil or Grill	1 1/2 to 2 hours
Ground Pork Patties	1/2"	Broil or Grill	8 to 10 minutes
Loin Chops or Cutlets	1/4" or 3/4"	Stove top	3 - 4 minutes or 7 - 8 minutes
Tenderloin Medallions	1/4"- 1/2"	Stove top	4 to 8 minutes
Ground Pork Patties	1/2"	Stove top	8 to 10 minutes
Chops, Cutlets, Cubes, Medallions	1/4" to 1"	Braise	10 to 25 minutes
Boston Butt, Boneless	3 - 6 lbs.	Braise	2 to 2 1/2 hours
Ribs, all types	2 - 4 lbs.	Braise	1 1/2 to 2 hours
Ribs, all types	2 to 4 lbs.	Stew	2 to 2 1/2 hours or until tender
Cubes	1"	Stew	45 to 60 minutes

NOTE: Cooking times compiled from various resources.

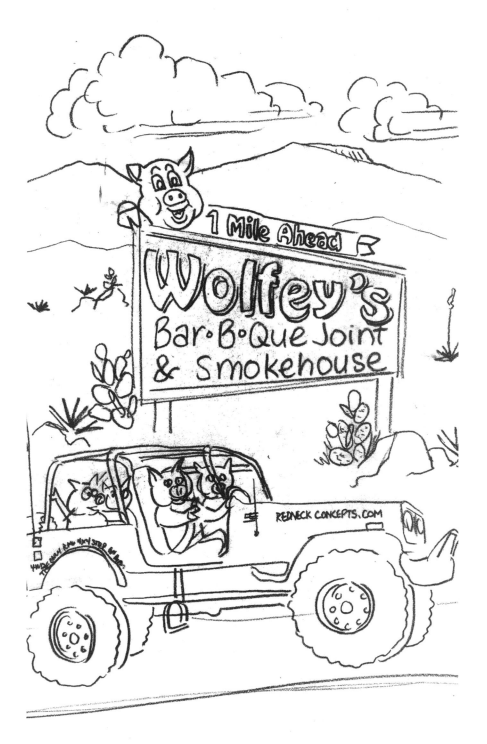

91

HINT: Who said that Chinese food had to be prepared in a wok? This recipe is prefect for the dutch oven or a skillet on the stovetop.

TIP: This recipe can be easily doubled or tripled and used for a big get-together at home. It is also a good one to take to a potluck dinner as well.

© 2006 Grant Reid

SESAME PORK WITH BROCCOLI
(CROWD PLEASER)

INGREDIENTS
1 can chicken broth
2 tbsp. cornstarch
1 tbsp. soy sauce
4 green onions, finely chopped
1 lb. pork tenderloin
1 tbsp. oil
1 tbsp. minced garlic
1 1/2 lbs. fresh broccoli or 1 bag
   frozen broccoli
2 tbsp. sliced pimiento, drained
   (small jar)
2 tbsp. sesame seed
1 bag boil-in-bag instant rice

TOOLS
knife
charcoal
large spoon
charcoal starter
hot mitts
dutch oven

Pre-prep: In small bowl combine chicken broth, cornstarch, soy sauce, and green onions. Put into zipper-style bag. Cut pork into 1-inch cubes. Heat oil over medium-high heat. Add pork and garlic. Stir-fry for 3-4 minutes. Set aside to cool. Place into a zipper-style bag. Cut fresh broccoli into bite-size pieces and place into a zipper bag or use 1 bag of frozen broccoli. Cook rice per packet directions. Let cool and place in a zipper-style bag. Measure out the pimientos and place in zipper-_____ (fill in blank). Place sesame seeds in zipper-style bag. Group and label.

Cooking method: Dutch oven. Use 1/2 the briquettes on the bottom and 1/2 the briquettes on the top. In dutch oven, toast sesame seeds. Remove seeds and add broccoli and broth mixture to oven. Cover and simmer for 10 minutes. Add cooked pork and pimiento. Cook just until mixture is hot, stirring frequently. Top with cooked rice and let cook 20 minutes. Sprinkle with sesame seeds and serve.

HINT: Who said that Chinese food had to be prepared in a wok? This recipe is prefect for the dutch oven or a skillet on the stovetop.

TIP: This recipe can be easily doubled or tripled and used for a big get-together at home. It is also a good one to take to a potluck dinner as well.

SESAME PORK WITH BROCCOLI
(CROWD PLEASER)

INGREDIENTS
1 can chicken broth
2 tbsp. cornstarch
1 tbsp. soy sauce
4 green onions, finely chopped
1 lb. pork tenderloin
1 tbsp. oil
1 tbsp. minced garlic
1 1/2 lbs. fresh broccoli or 1 bag
  frozen broccoli
2 tbsp. sliced pimiento, drained
  (small jar)
2 tbsp. sesame seed
1 bag boil-in-bag instant rice

TOOLS
stovetop over medium-high heat
knife
large skillet
medium bowl
large spoon

Pre-prep or Camp-prep: In medium bowl, combine chicken broth, cornstarch, soy sauce, and green onions. Set aside. Cut pork into 1-inch cubes. Cut fresh broccoli into bite-size pieces or use 1 bag of frozen broccoli.

Cooking method: Stovetop over medium-high heat. Cook rice per packet directions. Brown sesame seeds in skillet. Remove seeds. Heat oil over medium-high heat. Add pork and garlic. Stir-fry for 3-4 minutes. Remove pork. Add broccoli and broth mixture to skillet. Cover and simmer for 8 minutes. Add cooked pork and pimiento. Cook just until mixture is hot, stirring frequently (15 minutes). Sprinkle with sesame seeds and serve over rice.

HINT: This is one that not everyone will enjoy. It is not one of my favorites, but my better half loves it, and you don't want to get between her and the plate on this one.

TIP: Make this one at home first using the RV'ers Style and just try it, so that at camp, you and your friends or family are not disappointed. Try replacing rice with noodles.

ORANGE PORK

OFF-ROAD & CAMPING STYLE

INGREDIENTS

2 tbsp. olive or vegetable oil

1 1/2 pounds pork loin

1/2 lb. small mush-
rooms

2 med. onions, chopped

2 tbsp. minced garlic

2 tbsp. flour

1 cup dry white wine

1/2 cup orange juice

1/4 cup tomato paste

1/2 tsp. dried basil leaves

1/2 tsp. dried thyme
leaves

1/4 tsp. Tabasco sauce

1 chicken bouillon cube

1 bag boil-in-bag instant
rice

TOOLS

large spoon

charcoal starter

hot mitts

dutch oven

charcoal

Pre-prep: Cut pork into 1-inch cubes. Heat 1 tbsp. oil in skillet over med-high heat. Brown pork. Let cool. Place in a zipper-style bag. Chop onions. Place onion, mushrooms, and garlic into zipper-style bag. Cook rice per packet directions. Let cool. Place in a zipper-style bag. Measure flour into another zipper-style bag. In a medium bowl, combine orange juice, wine, tomato paste, basil, thyme, Tabasco sauce, and bouillon. Place into a zipper-style bag. Group and label.

Cooking method: Dutch oven. Use 1/2 the briquettes on the bottom and 1/2 the briquettes on the top. Using 1 tbsp. of oil, sauté onion, garlic, and mushrooms for about 5 minutes or until tender. Add pork. Heat for 5 minutes. Sprinkle in flour. Stirring constantly, cook for 3 minutes. Stir in liquid mixture slowly to prevent clumping. Simmer 1 hour, rotating every 15 minutes and stirring. The last 15 minutes, top with rice. Serve hot.

RV'ERS STYLE

TOOLS
stovetop over medium-high heat
large, heavy saucepan
medium bowl
large spoon

Pre-prep or Camp-prep: Cut pork into 1-inch cubes. Chop onions. In a medium bowl, combine orange juice, wine, tomato paste, basil, thyme, Tabasco sauce, and bouillon.

Cooking method: Stovetop over med-high heat. Heat 1 tbsp. oil in saucepan. Brown pork (5 minutes) add mushrooms, onions, and garlic sauté 5 minutes, until tender. Sprinkle with flour. Stir constantly; cook 3 minutes. Stir in liquid mixture slowly to prevent clumping. Cover; simmer 1 hour or until meat is tender. Stir occasionally. Boil rice per packet directions. Serve over rice.   97

HINT: When camping or off-roading, this recipe is pretty hard. I would recommend cooking this one in full and using the dutch oven or grill at camp to warm it up. For the RV'ers, well, it's up to you on this one.

TIP: For those of you who would like to change it up a little, the rice can be substituted using German sausage, jalapeño sausage, cornbread stuffing, etc. Stuff the leftover tenderloin with one of these choices for a test run. Or slice in thin strips, grill or sauté for manifold lunches (See Manifold Lunch Section). These are a few of my favorites.

STUFFED PORK TENDERLOIN
(MUST-TRY ITEM)

INGREDIENTS
1 whole pork tenderloin
1 lb. bacon
1 boil-in-bag rice (long grain wild)
2 oz. cream cheese
1/8 tsp. salt
1/8 tsp. pepper
1/8 tsp. Adobo

TOOLS
knife
foil
grill
charcoal starter
charcoal

Pre-prep: Cook rice per packet directions. Mix cream cheese and all spices to cooked rice while hot. Set aside. Unwrap tenderloin. You will want to use the large end of the loin. Cut loin 12" to 14" from large end. Set aside the small end and check out the tip for what you're going to do with that. Cut loin down the center from one end to the other (careful not to cut all the way through). You should now have a pocket, which you will stuff with the cooked rice mixture. Stuff well, without letting it overflow. Once you have finished that, it's time for the bacon. Starting at one end, wrap one piece of bacon so that the ends overlap on the bottom (the side you stuffed). On the next piece, do the same thing, only you will overlap half of the piece over the first, and the ends will overlap on the bottom. You will overlap each piece half over the previous piece, all the way to the other end. Place in foil-lined pan (stuffed side down). Cook in oven at 400 degrees for one hour. Remove. Using the foil, remove tenderloin from pan and place on a large sheet of foil. Wrap well, place in zipper-style bag. (Be careful not to spill juices.) Refrigerate or ice until ready to cook.

Cooking method: Grill. Use 20-25 briquettes. When coals are ready (gray), place foil-wrapped tenderloin directly over coals on grate. Cover and cook 30 minutes. Enjoy!

99

HINT: When camping or off-roading, this recipe is pretty hard. I would recommend cooking this one in full and using the dutch oven or grill at camp to warm it up. For the RV'ers, well, it's up to you on this one.

TIP: For those of you who would like to change it up a little, the rice can be substituted using German sausage, jalapeño sausage, cornbread stuffing, etc. Stuff the leftover tenderloin with one of these choices for a test run. Or slice in thin strips, grill or sauté for manifold lunches (See Manifold Lunch Section). These are a few of my favorites.

STUFFED PORK TENDERLOIN
(MUST-TRY ITEM)

INGREDIENTS
1 whole pork tenderloin
1 lb. bacon
1 boil-in-bag rice (long grain wild)
2 oz. cream cheese
1/8 tsp. salt
1/8 tsp. pepper
1/8 tsp. adobo

TOOLS
oven @ 400 degrees
knife
foil
9x13 metal pan

Pre-prep or Camp-prep: Cook rice per packet directions. Mix cream cheese and all spices into cooked rice while hot. Set aside. Unwrap tenderloin. You will want to use the large end of the loin. Cut loin 12" to 14" from large end. Set aside the small end and check out the tip for what you're going to do with that. Cut loin down the center from one end to the other (careful not to cut all the way through). You should now have a pocket, which you will stuff with the cooked rice mixture. Stuff well, without letting it overflow. Once you have finished that, it's time for the bacon. Starting at one end, wrap one piece of bacon so that the ends overlap on the bottom (the side you stuffed). On the next piece, do the same thing, only you will overlap half of the piece over the first and the ends will overlap on the bottom. You will overlap each piece half over the previous piece, all the way to the other end. Place in zipper-style bag or place in foil-lined pan.

Cooking method: Oven @ 400 degrees. This is the easy part; just throw it in the oven for 60 minutes and you will have a mouth-watering stuffed pork tenderloin ready to eat.

HINT: You know what they say "The Sauce Is The Boss"; well, in this case, it couldn't be more true. Please choose a sauce that everyone will enjoy (not too hot, not too sweet).

TIP: There are two ways to prepare this recipe in this cookbook. Both ways are very good; it just depends on how much time and maintenance you want to deal with. The dutch oven or oven is little to no maintenance.

BAKED-UP BABY BACKS

OFF-ROAD & CAMPING STYLE

INGREDIENTS
1 rack baby back ribs
2 cups BBQ sauce (Sweet
   Baby Ray's)
1/2 tsp. pepper
1/4 tsp. salt
1/4 tsp. Adobo
1/2 tbsp. fresh chopped garlic

TOOLS
dutch oven
charcoal
charcoal starter
hot mitts
tongs

Pre-prep: Cut rack of ribs in half and boil in large soup pot for 15 minutes. (This will ensure that they will melt in your mouth.) Once complete, let cool and cut them into individual ribs and place in large zipper-style bag. Add the rest of the ingredients to the bag: BBQ sauce, salt, pepper, adobo, and garlic. Mix well and refrigerate or ice until ready to cook.

Cooking method: Dutch oven. Use 1/3 briquettes on the bottom and 2/3 briquettes on the lid. Place the ribs and all contents of zipper-style bag in dutch oven and bake for 40 minutes, rotating oven every 15 minutes, stirring each time. Enjoy!

RV'ERS STYLE

TOOLS
oven @ 350 degrees
9x13 metal pan
large soup pot
large spoon

Camp-prep: Cut rack of ribs in half and boil in large soup pot for 15 minutes. (This will ensure that they will melt in your mouth.) Once ribs have parboiled, cut ribs so that they are individual pieces. Place in foil-lined pan and add the ingredients: BBQ sauce, salt, pepper, adobo, and garlic. Stir well so that all the ribs are coated.

Cooking method: Oven @ 350 degrees. This is the easy part; just place them in the oven for 50 minutes, stirring every 15 minutes. Enjoy!

HINT: Try to use bone-in pork chops that are about 1" thick. That gives the potatoes a chance to cook. If you use thin chops, they will cook much quicker than the potatoes.

TIP: If you are cooking the crusted chops in an oven and are not using potatoes, try to use a wire rack to keep them off the bottom of the pan. This will help to make the outside of the chop crisp.

CRUSTED BONE-IN CHOPS

OFF-ROAD & CAMPING STYLE

INGREDIENTS
4 - 1"-thick bone-in pork chops
2 cups corn flakes (crushed)
1 cup milk
10 - #1 new potatoes
2 tbsp. oil
1/8 tsp. pepper
1/8 tsp. salt
1/8 tsp. Adobo
1 pinch garlic power

TOOLS
dutch oven
charcoal
charcoal starter
hot mitts
tongs
knife

Pre-prep: Start by placing chops, corn flakes, milk, and oil in separate zipper-style bags (no generics). All the spices go together in one bag. Cut new potatoes into quarters and place in zipper-style bag and cover with water to prevent browning. You know the routine; all the bags in one large bag, group and label.

Cooking method: Dutch oven. Use 1/3 of briquettes on the bottom and 2/3 of briquettes on the lid. Start by one at a time dipping the chops in the milk and then in the corn flakes. You will want to mash the corn flakes into the chops so they get coated well. Drain potatoes. Heat oven 3 minutes and add oil. Place potatoes in the bottom so that they make somewhat of a flat surface, and sprinkle with spices. On top of the potatoes, you will put the chops. Cover and bake 40-50 minutes. Rotating every 15 minutes.

RV'ERS STYLE

TOOLS
oven @ 400 degrees
baking pan
knife
hot pad holder

Camp-prep: Start by one at a time dipping the chops in the milk and then in the corn flakes. You will want to mash the corn flakes into the chops so they get coated well. Place in pan. Cut potatoes in quarters and toss with 2 tbsp. oil, then place them around the chops so that are touching the bottom of the pan (the roasted effect).

Cooking method: Oven @ 400 degrees. Place in oven and bake for 40 minutes, or until crisp and brown. Making me hungry!

105

HINT: When starting the grill, be sure to use plenty of starter fluid. Most of the fluids call for 1.6 oz. of fluid per 1 lb. of charcoal, which is 1 1/2 shot glasses. Once the coals are completely gray, all the fluid will have burned off.

TIP: By waiting until the ribs are almost done (last 10 minutes) before putting on the sauce, this will prevent the sauce from burning and turning black. Once you have started the sauce process, you will want to keep turning and brushing more sauce (about once every minute), and I would say maybe repeat this four or five times or until well-coated with sauce.

GRILLED BABY BACK RIBS

OFF-ROAD, CAMPING, & RV'ERS STYLE

INGREDIENTS
1 rack baby back ribs
2 cup BBQ sauce (Sweet Baby Ray's)
1/2 tsp. pepper
1/4 tsp. salt
1/4 tsp. Adobo
1/2 tbsp. fresh chopped garlic

TOOLS
grill/campfire/grate
charcoal
charcoal starter
hot mitts
tongs
sauce brush

Pre-prep: Cut rack of ribs in half and boil in large soup pot for 15 minutes (this will insure that they will melt in your mouth). Coat both halves with spices. Let cool and place the two halves in a large _____ - ____ (fill in the blanks) bag. Put the sauce in a zipper-style bag or you can take the bottle, but keep it grouped with the meal. Spices all together in one, that's right, all together in one large zipper-style bag. Gruop and label.

Cooking method: Grill. Use 20-25 briquettes. Once coals are ready, it's time for the ribs. Place them directly over the coals. Turn every 4-5 minutes, but no sauce yet! Continue this process for 25 minutes, then take your sauce and brush (and sauce and brush). You need to be on top of things here; you will want to turn these jewels about once every minute so that the sauce does not burn. Repeat this until you have coated each side 4-5 times (the more the merrier).

107

HINT: This is another one where you will want to buy chops that are at least 1" thick, and I would recommend using bone-in chops. When cutting the slit in the chop, preparing to stuff, please be careful not to cut yourself by running the knife through the side of the chop.

TIP: Depending on the size of the chops, you may have leftover stuffing. If so, go ahead and plan on having stuffed mushrooms. Not necessarily with this meal, but sometime during the outing.

STUFFED PORK CHOPS
(USE BAKED STUFFED MUSHROOM STUFFING)

OFF-ROAD & CAMPING STYLE

INGREDIENTS

4-1"-thick bone-in
  pork chops
2 c. stuffing (use baked
  stuffed mushroom
  stuffing)
1/4 tsp. salt & pepper

1/8 tsp. adobo
10 #1 or #2 new
   potatoes
2 tbsp. oil

TOOLS

dutch oven
charcoal
charcoal starter
hot mitts
tongs
skewers

Pre-prep: Stand chops on end, fat strip down. Slice starting in the center of the chop, leaving about 1/2" of meat not sliced. You will have a pocket the shape of the chop. Prepare the stuffing. Using the baked stuffed mushroom recipe. Now stuff, baby! Each chop will take about 1/2 cup of stuffing. Pinch the opening closed and secure with skewer (break off excess skewer). Place in zipper-style bag. Cut potatoes into quarters and throw 'em in a zipper-style bag, cover with water to prevent _____(fill in blank). Group and label.

Cooking method: Dutch oven. Use 1/3 briquettes on the bottom and 2/3 briquettes on the lid. Heat oven 3 minutes and add oil. Place potatoes in the bottom so that they make somewhat of a flat surface, and sprinkle with spices. Place chops on top of potatoes. Cover and bake 30-40 minutes, rotating every 15 minutes.

RV'ERS STYLE

TOOLS
oven @ 400 degrees
baking pan
knife
hot pad holder

Pre-prep or Camp-prep: Stand chops on end, fat strip down. Slice starting in the center of the chop, leaving about 1/2" of meat not sliced. You'll have a pocket the shape of the chop. Prepare the stuffing (using the baked stuffed mushroom recipe. Now stuff, baby! Each chop will take about 1/2 cup stuffing. Pinch the opening closed and secure with skewer (break off excess skewer) and place in baking pan. Cut potatoes in quarters and toss with 2 tbsp. oil. Then place them around the chops so that are touching the bottom of the pan (the roasted effect).

Cooking method: Oven @ 400 degrees. Place in oven and bake for 35-45 minutes, until brown and potatoes are tender. Enjoy!

109

Food Quantities (25, 50 and 100 Servings)

Food	25	50	100
Rolls	4 dozen	8 dozen	16 dozen
Bread	50 slices	100 slices	200 slices
Butter	1/2 pound	1 pound	1 1/2 pounds
Mayonnaise	1 cup	2 - 3 cups	4 - 6 cups
Jams	1 1/2 pounds	3 pounds	6 pounds
Crackers	1 1/2 pounds	3 pounds	6 pounds
Cheese	3 pounds	6 pounds	12 pounds
Soup	1 1/2 gallons	3 gallons	6 gallons
Salad Dressing	1 pint	2 1/2 pints	1/2 gallon
Meat, Poultry, Fish:			
Wieners	6 1/2 pounds	13 pounds	25 pounds
Hamburger	9 pounds	18 pounds	35 pounds
Turkey or Chicken	13 pounds	25 - 35 pounds	50 - 75 pounds
Fish, Whole	13 pounds	25 pounds	50 pounds
Fish, Fillet or Steak	7 1/2 pounds	15 pounds	30 pounds
Salads, Casseroles, Vegetables:			
Potato Salad	4 1/4 quarts	2 1/4 gallons	4 1/2 gallons
Scalloped Potatoes	4 1/2 quarts	8 1/2 quarts	17 quarts
Mashed Potatoes	9 pounds	16- 20 pounds	25 - 35 pounds
Spaghetti	1 1/4 gallons	2 1/2 gallons	6 gallons
Baked Beans	3/4 gallon	1 1/4 gallons	2 1/2 gallons
Jello Salad	3/4 gallon	1 1/4 gallons	2 1/2 gallons
Canned Vegetables	1 #10 can	2 1/2 #10 cans	4 #10 cans
Fresh Vegetables:			
Lettuce	4 heads	8 heads	15 heads
Carrots	6 1/4 pounds	12 1/2 pounds	25 pounds
Tomatoes	3 - 5 pounds	7 - 10 pounds	14 - 20 pounds
Desserts:			
Watermelon	37 1/2 pounds	75 pounds	150 pounds
Fruit Cup	3 quarts	6 quarts	12 quarts
Cake, Sheet	1 - 10x12"	1 - 12x20"	2 - 12x20"
Cake, Layer	1 1/2 - 10"	3 - 10"	8 - 10"
Whip Cream	3/4 pint	1 1/2 - 2 pints	3 pints

111

HINT: Fish, to some people, is very hard to cook and has a tendency to be overcooked. (I have that problem anyway.) This tilapia will only take about 2 to 2 1/2 minutes on each side. If overcooked, it will become dry.

TIP: The reason I have suggested frozen crawfish is 1) crawfish, depending on where you live, are not always available, and 2) it takes a lot of time to get 8 oz. of tail meat, not to mention you still have to cook them.

GRILLED BLACKENED TILAPIA
W/ A CAJUN CRAWFISH SAUCE

INGREDIENTS
4 tilapia filets
1 tbsp. Blackened Red Fish
  Magic (seasoning)
cajun crawfish sauce (see basic white
  sauce in side dish section)
8-oz. pkg. frozen crawfish tail meat,
  pre-cooked and ready to eat

TOOLS
grill/campfire/grate
campstove
charcoal
charcoal starter
spatula
sauce pot

Pre-prep: Coat your filets with the seasoning and place them in a zipper-style bag. Prepare the sauce using the Basic White Sauce recipe in the Side Dish Section, adding the crawfish tail meat and Blackened Redfish Magic at the end when sauce has become smooth. Once completed with your sauce, let cool and place (you guessed it) in a zipper-style bag. Group and label.

Cooking method: Grill. Use 15-20 briquettes. As soon as you start the grill, you will want to start boiling the water to heat the sauce. Boil 10 minutes; the filets will only take about 2 1/2 minutes on each side over hot coals. Any longer and the fish may be dry. Serve with 3/4 cup of Cajun Crawfish Sauce atop the filets. Very tasty!

HINT: Fresh shrimp are best, but not always available. The bigger the better on this one (9 to 12 count). I use three shrimp per skewer and prepare two skewers per person.

TIP: When putting the shrimp on the skewer, lay shrimp flat on a surface; go through the tail and then put a piece of pineapple on and then go through the top part. The end result will be that there is a piece of pineapple in between the shrimp. When the shrimp is cooked, it will shrink and the pineapple stays in the shrimp when served.

GRILLED PINEAPPLE SHRIMP

INGREDIENTS
24 large shrimp (6-9 count)
12 oz. can pineapple chunks
2 large green peppers
2 large red peppers
1 large red onion
8 oz. orange juice
1/2 cup brown sugar
10 oz. fresh mushrooms

TOOLS
grill/campfire/grate
charcoal
charcoal starter
tongs
skewers

Pre-prep: Cut all veggies in 1" cubes and peel shrimp, all but the tail (makes a good handle). Start filling up the skewers. (See Tip.) Once all the skewers are complete, place a mushroom on each end and place in zipper-style bag. In a saucepan, heat orange juice to a boil and add brown sugar, stirring constantly until sugar is melted. Set aside and let cool. Can you guess what's next? Yep, place in zipper-style bag. Group and label.

Cooking method: Grill. Use 20-25 briquettes. When coals are ready, place skewers directly over coals. Grill 11/2 minutes on first side, turn and baste with orange juice glaze. Grill 11/2 minutes and turn again, basting. Repeat this process 3-4 more times to ensure that the glaze gets sticky. Enjoy!

HINT: Fresh shrimp are best, but not always available. The bigger the better on this one (9 to 12 count). I use three shrimp per skewer and prepare two skewers per person.

TIP: By waiting until the shrimp and veggies are almost done before putting on the sauce, this will prevent the sauce from burning and turning black. Once you have started the sauce process, you will want to keep turning and brushing more sauce (about once every 30 seconds) and repeat this 4 or 5 times or until well-coated with sauce.

GRILLED PINEAPPLE BBQ SHRIMP

INGREDIENTS
24 large shrimp (6-9 count)
12 oz. can pineapple chunks
2 large green peppers
2 large red peppers
1 large red onion
12 oz. bottle BBQ sauce
10 oz. cherry tomatoes

TOOLS
grill/campfire/grate
charcoal
charcoal starter
tongs
skewers
sauce brush

Pre-prep: Cut all veggies in 1" cubes and peel shrimp, all but the tail (makes a good handle). Start filling up the skewers. (See Tip.) Once all the skewers are complete, place cherry tomato on each end and place in zipper-style bag. Place all ingredients in large zipper-style bag and label.

Cooking method: Grill. Use 20-25 briquettes. When coals are ready, place skewers directly over coals. Grill 11/2 minutes on first side, turn and baste with BBQ sauce. Grill 11/2 minutes and turn again, basting. Repeat this process 3-4 more times to ensure that the BBQ sauce gets sticky. Enjoy!

Note: You have probably already noticed that the only thing different in this recipe from the one before it is that one has BBQ sauce and the other one is orange glaze. However, the two tastes could not be further apart.

HINT: If your going to shuck your own oysters, make sure that they are fresh from a good source (don't buy oysters by the sea in July) and when shucking, do not use any oyster whose shell is open. There is a good possibility that it is no good.

TIP: RV'ers, when using an oven, large shell halves (which may be purchased at any specialty cook store) work well for individual servings.

OYSTERS ROCKEFELLER

OFF-ROAD & CAMPING STYLE

INGREDIENTS
2 - 10-oz. packages chopped
    frozen spinach
1 cup water
1/2 cup chopped onion
1 tbsp. chopped garlic
2 tbsp. butter
1/4 tsp. Adobo seasoning
16 oz. jar oysters (shucked)
1 cup parmesan cheese

TOOLS
dutch oven
charcoal
charcoal starter
hot mitts
tongs
cold beverage
saucepot

Pre-prep: Clean oysters well with water. Place in zipper-style bag. Boil spinach, onion, garlic, butter, and adobo in water 20 minutes drain well (no liquid). Place in zipper-style bag. Prepare parmesan white sauce in the side dish section and place in zipper-style bag. Group and label.

Cooking method: Dutch oven. Use 1/3 briquettes on the bottom and 2/3 briquettes on the lid. Put spinach in bottom of dutch oven; spread evenly. Space out oysters on top of spinach and then cover with parmesan cheese. Bake 25-30 minutes until cheese is brown. Boil water in saucepot to heat the parmesan cheese sauce. Boil 10-15 minutes; serve with sauce on top and crackers.

RV'ERS STYLE

TOOLS
stovetop
oven @ 350 degrees
6x9 baking pan
whisk
saucepot
hot pad holder

Camp-prep: Clean oysters well with water. Boil spinach, onion, garlic, butter, and adobo in water 20 minutes; drain well (no liquid).

Cooking method: Oven @ 350 degrees. Make a bed of spinach in the bottom of the pan and top with oysters. Cover with cheese and bake 25-30 minutes. While you're waiting for the oysters to finish, you can make your parmesan cheese sauce in the side dish section. Serve oysters topped with sauce and crackers.

HINT: Make sure that when you're planning on catching your fish, please take a few cans of Beanie-Weenies or soup. My experience has been that we only end up having fish about once out of every three or four camping trips, and yes it is on the menu every trip.

TIP: Let trout soak in milk for 15 minutes or so, and it will take a little of the strong fish taste right out. No longer than 25 minutes, or fish will become soggy.

GRILLED ROCKY MOUNTAIN TROUT

OFF-ROAD, CAMPING, & RV'ERS STYLE

INGREDIENTS
4-6 medium trout
1 stick butter (cut into 6 equals)
2 lemon (cut in 12 pieces)
2 oranges (cut in 12 pieces)
3 tbsp. oil
1/2 tsp. pepper
1/2 tsp. salt
1/2 tsp. Adobo
1/2 tsp. garlic powder

TOOLS
grill/campfire/grate
charcoal
charcoal starter
foil
fishing pole

Pre-prep: Cut fruit in wedges so that you have 12 pieces of each fruit, and place in separate zipper-style bags. All the spices go in one bag. Oil goes in another. And if you have already caught your trout, you can put them in a zipper-style bag too. Group and label.

Cooking method: Grill. U se 20-25 briquettes. Start grill. Start by getting 4-6 pieces of foil about 18" long. Place a whole trout on each piece of foil. Using 2 lemon and 2 orange wedges on each trout, squeeze over top. Spices go on top of that, and then the butter on top of the spices. Wrap in foil so that there is an air pocket inside. Grill covered 15-20 minutes or until fish is flaky.

HINT: This is a very colorful dish and is very pretty and appetizing when sitting on a plate in front of you. Try this recipe one night when you have company over for dinner.

TIP: If serving this dish for friends, take two minutes and cut some garnish, an orange slice about 1/2" thick round and from center cut out to one side, so it can be twisted to somewhat of an arch. Place cherry and parsley beside orange on top of sauce.

SHRIMP BATON ROUGE

OFF-ROAD & CAMPING STYLE

INGREDIENTS
24 large shrimp (6-9 count)
1 green pepper
1 red pepper
1 yellow pepper
1 red onion
2 tbsp. olive oil
1/2 tbsp. garlic
cajun white sauce
1 package fettuccine noodles

TOOLS
camp stove
hot mitt
big spoon
foil
large skillet

Pre-prep: Peel and de-vein shrimp. Put shrimp and garlic into a zipper-style bag. Cut peppers and onion into strips. Put in zipper-style bag. Make Cajun white sauce as directed in the Side Dish Section. Let cool. Put into zipper-style bag. Boil fettuccine as directed on package. Let cool. Place in zipper-style bag. Group and label.

Cooking method: Camp stove over medium-high heat. Sauté garlic and shrimp in skillet using 1 tbsp. oil. Remove and keep warm in foil, tightly sealed. Sauté peppers and onions in 1 tbsp. oil. Remove and place in separate foil, tightly sealed. Heat sauce and noodles in boiling water until hot. To serve: Place noodles on bottom. Top with shrimp, then peppers, then with sauce. Serve immediately.

RV'ERS STYLE

TOOLS
stovetop
big spoon
large saucepan
large skillet
foil
hot pad holder

Camp-prep: Peel and de-vein shrimp. Cut peppers and onion into strips.

Cooking method: Stove top. Sauté garlic and shrimp in large skillet. Remove and keep warm in foil, tightly sealed. Sauté peppers and onion in same skillet. Remove and place in separate foil, tightly sealed. Make Cajun white sauce in the side dish section. Add noodles in boiling water. Cook as directed. To serve: Place noodles on bottom. Top with shrimp, then peppers, then with sauce. Serve immediately.

123

SPICE AND HERB GUIDE

ALLSPICE: This is from a very small fruit that comes from Mexico, Jamaica, Central and South American. Usually used in pickles. It can also be used in meats, boiled fish, gravies (ground) relishes and fruit preserves.

BASIL: This is from a leaf of an herb grown in U.S. or the Mediterranean area. Used in poultry or lamb, tomato dishes, soups. Also in cooked peas, snap beans and squash.

BAY LEAVES: This is from a leaf of an evergreen that is grown in the eastern Mediterranian area. Used in a variety of meat, fish, soups, stews and sauces.

CARAWAY: This is a seed of a plant that is grown in the Netherlands. Used in cheese spreads, baking breads, noodles and sauerkraut. You can and also use it to zest up french fried potatoes, canned asparagus or liver.

CURRY POWDER: This is a blend of as many as 16-20 spices ground together. Used in all Indian curry dishes. Lamb, chicken, eggs, rice and vegetables.

DILL: This is a seed from the dill plant that is grown in India. Used in cooked macarrón, potato salad, sauerkraut and pickling recipes.

MACE: This is the covering on a nutmeg seed. Used whole in fish, fish sauces, stewed fruit and pickling. Used ground in pastries, doughnuts and baked goods. Mace adds a unusual flavor to chocolate desserts.

MARJORAM: This is an herb from the mint family and is grown in France and Chile. Used in soups, sauces, stews and beverages. Try spinkling on a lamb before roasting.

OREGANO: This is a plant from the mint family and a spicies of the marjoram. Used in Italian specialties, pizza, chile carne and any tomato dish.

PAPARIKA: This is a from a sweet pepper and is grown in the U.S., Central Europe and Spain. Used in salad dressings, chicken and goulash. It is also used as a garnish to put color in pale foods such as deviled eggs or potato salad.

POPPY: This is a seed from a flower that is grown in Holland. Used to top rolls, breads and cookies. It has a nutty like flavor.

ROSEMARY: This is a herb that looks like pine needles and is grown in Portugal, Spain and France. Used to sweeten soups, stews and to spinkle on beef or lamb before roasting.

SAGE: This is a leaf from a shrub grown in Albania, Yugoslavia and Greece. Used in salads, stews, hamburgers, meat loaf, sausages and a stuffing in meat or poultry.

THYME: This is a leaf from a shrub that is grown in Spain and France. Used to season poultry, fish dishes and fresh sliced tomatoes.

TURMERIC: This is a root from the ginger family that is grown in Peru, Jamaica, Haiti and India. Used to flavor and as a coloring in prepared mustard and in combination with mustard in salads, dressings and meats.

125

HINT: Don't be scared by the idea of making a sauce from scratch; just follow the directions and you may even surprise yourself. Super easy.

TIP: Whatever you do, don't walk away from this at any time. You must baby-sit and stir constantly. Make sure that flour and butter are mixed well with no lumps before adding the milk. For a darker sauce, cook the flour and butter mixture longer (the longer it cooks, the darker it will be). For a beef-based sauce wait until pretty dark and use water instead of milk, and add 1 tbsp. beef base (great brown gravy).

BASIC WHITE SAUCE

OFF-ROAD & CAMPING STYLE

INGREDIENTS
3 tbsp. butter
2 tbsp. flour
2 cups milk
1/4 tsp. salt
1/4 tsp. pepper
1 tbsp. water

TOOLS
medium pan
whisk

Pre-prep: Melt butter. Add flour, stirring constantly until well-mixed and there are no lumps. Gradually add milk. Continue stirring. The sauce will start to thicken. Add salt and pepper. Add water. Let cool and place in a zipper-style bag.

Sausage Gravy Recipe - Cook 1 lb. ground country sausage. Add to basic white sauce. (See biscuits and sausage gravy recipe.)

Parmesan Cheese Sauce - Follow Basic White Sauce recipe and add 1/2 cup parmesan cheese. (See Oysters Rockefeller recipe.)

Cajun Sauce - Follow basic white sauce recipe and add 1/2 tsp. Blackened Redfish Magic Cajun seasoning. (See Shrimp Baton Rouge recipe.)

Cajun Crawfish Sauce - Follow basic white sauce recipe and add 1/2 tsp. Blackened Redfish Magic Cajun seasoning and crawfish. (See grilled blackened tilapia with a Cajun crawfish recipe.)

Cooking method: Place freezer-style zipper bag in boiling water to heat. Boil 15 minutes.

RV'ERS STYLE

TOOLS
medium pan
whisk

Pre-prep or Camp-prep: If you don't pre-prep, just start with the cooking method.

Cooking method: Stovetop over medium heat. Melt butter. Add flour, stirring constantly until well-mixed and there are no lumps. Gradually add milk. Continue stirring. The sauce will start to thicken. Add salt and pepper. Add water.

HINT: These little jewels are an excellent addition to any meal and if you want to jazz it up a little, check out the short but sweet tip.

TIP: Instead of using the parmesan cheese, use a cheddar/Monterey jack blend cheese and the chili recipe in the soups, salads, stews, and chili section. Cook potatoes as directed, and then add the chili and then the cheese and bake another 15 minutes until chili is warm and cheese is melted. Enjoy.

PARMESAN POTATOES

OFF-ROAD & CAMPING STYLE

INGREDIENTS
4 medium red potatoes
1 small onion
3 tbsp. butter
1 1/2 cups parmesan cheese
1/4 tsp. salt
1/8 tsp. pepper
1/2 tsp. garlic powder

TOOLS
dutch oven
large spoon
charcoal
starter fluid
hot mitts
knife

Pre-prep: Cut potatoes in thin slices about 1/8". Put in zipper-style bag and add water to prevent browning. Cut onions into thin slices and separate into rings. Put onions in zipper-style bag. Measure salt, pepper, and garlic powder in a separate zipper-style bag. Keep parmesan cheese in original bag. Group and label.

Cooking method: Dutch oven. Use 1/3 briquettes on the bottom and 2/3 briquettes on the lid. Melt butter. Remove butter; keep on hand to drizzle over potatoes. Place half the potatoes in bottom. Onion rings go on top of that, the other half of the potatoes on top of the onions. Drizzle with butter. Sprinkle on the parmesan cheese and seasoning. Cook 30-35 minutes.

RV'ERS STYLE

TOOLS
oven @ 400 degrees
2-quart baking dish
large spoon
knife
hot pad holder

Camp-prep: Cut potatoes in thin slices. Cut onions into thin slices and separate into rings. Grease baking dish. Place half of the potato slices in the dish. Top with onions and then the rest of the potatoes. Melt butter and drizzle over potatoes. Add a layer of parmesan cheese and sprinkle salt, pepper, and garlic powder over top.

Cooking method: Oven @ 400 degrees. Bake uncovered for 25 minutes or until potatoes are golden brown and tender.

HINT: This is a crowd-pleaser that everyone likes (and if you don't, well I'm sorry, you're missing out) and is simple to make. It can be prepped 4-5 days before needed and stores well.

TIP: When at home, if you want to get fancy, try using a pastry bag with a flower tip (instead of stuffing skins) and squeeze out half-dollar-size little flowers onto parchment paper and bake 15 minutes or until golden brown.

TWICE-BAKED POTATOES

OFF-ROAD & CAMPING STYLE

INGREDIENTS
2 large baking potatoes
2 tbsp. butter
1/4 cup milk
2 tbsp. sour cream
2 tbsp. chives or green onions
1/4 cup or 4 slices bacon
1/4 cup cheese
salt
pepper

TOOLS
dutch oven
starter fluid
charcoal
knife

Pre-prep: Bake potatoes for about 45 minutes at 400 degrees or until done. Let cool slightly (enough so that you can hold them in your hand). Slice potatoes in half. Scoop out with a spoon and put filling into mixing bowl. Set skins aside for later. Add milk, butter, and sour cream to bowl. Whip until smooth. Add chives, bacon, cheese, salt, and pepper. Mix well. Fill skins with equal parts of stuffing. Place in a zipper-style bag.

Cooking method: Dutch oven. Use 1/3 of the briquettes on the bottom and 2/3 of the briquettes on the lid. Place potatoes in dutch oven. Cook 30 minutes, rotating after 15 minutes.

RV'ERS STYLE

TOOLS
oven @ 400 degrees
foil
mixing bowl
mixer
knife

Pre-prep or Camp-prep: Oven @ 400 degrees. Bake potatoes for about 45 minutes or until done. Let cool slightly (so that you can hold them in your hand). Slice potato in half. Scoop out with a spoon and put filling into mixing bowl. Set skins aside for filling later. Add milk, butter, and sour cream to bowl. Mix until smooth. Add chives, bacon, cheese, salt, and pepper. Stir well. Fill skins with equal parts of stuffing. Keep in fridge until ready to cook.

Cooking method: Oven @ 400 degrees. Bake for about 30 minutes or until top is slightly crispy. Enjoy!

HINT: The cooking time for the veggies is personal preference as to whether you like crisp or soft (well-done) - 10 minutes for crisp and 20 for well-done and well, 15 minutes for in-between.

TIP: When opening the foil, the steam will be very hot, so please look at the veggies after you have opened the foil, as opposed to while you're opening the foil.

STEAMED VEGGIE SACK

INGREDIENTS
1 green pepper
1 red pepper
1 red onion
1 zucchini
1 yellow squash
1 small crown broccoli
1/2 tsp. pepper
1/4 tsp. salt
1/2 tsp. adobo
1 tbsp. minced garlic
3 tbsp. butter (optional)
1 tbsp. water

TOOLS
grill/campfire/grate
charcoal
charcoal starter
foil
hot mitts

Pre-prep: Cut all veggies into bite-size pieces, or they can be julienne (cut lengthways). All the veggies can be put into a _____ - _____ (fill in blanks) bag. If you are using both butter and water, they can be placed in the same bag. Place all dry spices in the same zipper-style bag. And the garlic can go with the veggies. Group and label.

Cooking method: Grill. If this is your only course to be cooked on the grill, you will need 15-20 briquettes, otherwise put them on with the other part of your meal. When coals become hot, you're almost ready. You need a piece of foil about 24" long. Place veggies in center of foil. Using ends of foil, hold them up and start rolling them together downward, leaving about 4" for air flow. Close the ends by rolling so that it is sealed well. Place over hot coals and cook 10-20 minutes (watch the steam when opening).

133

HINT: My kids Josh and Samantha don't really care for beans of any kind, but what's funny is that I can wrap these baked beans in a tortilla and they will eat the whole bowl, knowing they are eating beans.

TIP: The baked beans can also be prepared on the camp stove over medium heat and covered with foil for 20 minutes, stirring every 5 minutes.

BAKED BEANS WITH A KISS

INGREDIENTS
1 can Bush's baked beans
1 small onion
1/2 cup brown sugar (the kiss part)
1/4 cup ketchup
1 tbsp. mustard
1 tbsp. garlic
1/8 tsp. pepper
1/8 tsp. adobo

TOOLS
dutch oven
charcoal
charcoal starter
hot mitts
tongs
spoon

Pre-prep: Chop onions to a small dice. Onions and garlic can go together in the same zipper-style bag. The mustard, ketchup, and brown sugar all go in one bag. Not least but last, the spices together in one zipper-style bag. Group and label.

Cooking method: Dutch oven: Using 1/3 briquettes on the bottom and 2/3 briquettes on the lid. Put your baked beans in the dutch oven and add all ingredients and stir well. Cook 30-40 minutes and serve hot.

RV'ERS STYLE

TOOLS
oven @ 350 degrees
small casserole dish
spoon
hot pad holder

Camp-prep: Chop your onions to a small dice. Dice garlic (if you did not buy fresh minced garlic in a jar).

Cooking method: Oven @ 350 degrees. Place beans and all ingredients in small casserole dish. Stir well and place in oven. Bake 30 minutes. Enjoy!

HINT: After finishing dinner and relaxing around a campfire or just sitting under your awning, talking about the day's events, you will be WONDERING where all that noise is coming from. And now you know why we call them the Iowa 3 Bean Wonder.

TIP: This makes for a really good holiday, potluck, or picnic dish, with little to no effort. Can also be warmed in microwave with approved container.

IOWA 3 BEAN WONDER
(IOWA? IT'S JUST THE NAME.)

OFF-ROAD & CAMPING STYLE

INGREDIENTS	TOOLS
1/2 lb. ground beef	dutch oven
1/2 lb. bacon	charcoal
1 small onion	charcoal starter
1 can kidney beans	hot mitts
1 can pork and beans	tongs
1 can butter beans	spoon
1/3 c. brown sugar	knife
1/3 c. white sugar	
1/4 c. catsup	
1/2 tsp. mustard	

Pre-prep: Brown ground beef and bacon. Drain fat. Put in zipper-style bag. Chop onions to a small dice. Onions and garlic can go together in the same zipper-style bag. The mustard, ketchup, brown sugar and sugar all go in one bag. Not least but last, the spices go together in one zipper-style bag. Group and label.

Cooking method: Dutch oven. Use 1/2 the briquettes on the bottom and 1/2 the briquettes on the lid. Put all beans in the dutch oven and add all ingredients and stir well. Cook 40-50 minutes; serve hot.

RV'ERS STYLE

TOOLS
oven @ 350 degrees
casserole dish
spoon
frying pan
knife

Camp-prep: Brown ground beef and bacon. Drain fat. Chop onions to a small dice.

Cooking method: Oven @ 350 degrees. Put all beans in the casserole dish or Crock Pot. Add all ingredients and stir well. Bake for 1 hour or leave in Crock Pot while enjoying the day outdoors. Serve hot.

HINT: If you haven't noticed yet, in this cookbook, we don't count calories, have any diet recipes or fat intake charts. You're on vacation; come on, live it up, or should I say eat it up. That being said, you have to make the twice-baked sweet potatoes for one of your first sides.

TIP: These babies will be a lot like the quick cherry/apple/ blueberry cobbler and be very hot when they come out of the oven and will stick to little fingers. Please let cool 5 minutes before serving.

TWICE-BAKED SWEET POTATOES

OFF-ROAD & CAMPING STYLE

INGREDIENTS
2 large sweet potatoes
2 tbsp. butter
mini-marshmallows
1/8 tsp. nutmeg
1/8 tsp. cinnamon
1 tbsp. brown sugar

TOOLS
dutch oven
starter fluid
charcoal
knife

Pre-prep: Bake potatoes for about 30 minutes @ 400 degrees or until done. (Sweet potatoes don't take as long to bake as baking potatoes.) Let cool slightly (enough so that you can hold them in your hand). Slice potato in half. Scoop out with a spoon and put filling into mixing bowl. Set skins aside for filling later. Add milk, butter, nutmeg, cinnamon, and brown sugar to bowl. Mix until smooth. Fill skins with equal parts of stuffing. Let cool. Place in a zipper-style bag.

Cooking method: Dutch oven. Use 1/3 briquettes on the bottom 2/3 briquettes on the lid. Place potatoes in dutch oven. Cook 30 minutes, rotating after 15 minutes. Add mini-marshmallows and cook 10 minutes. Serve and enjoy!

RV'ERS STYLE

TOOLS
foil
mixing bowl
mixer
knife
oven @ 400 degrees

Pre-prep or Camp-prep: Oven @ 400 degrees. Bake potatoes for 30 minutes or until done. Let cool slightly (enough so that you can hold them in your hand). Slice potato in half. Scoop out with a spoon and put filling into mixing bowl. Set skins aside for filling later. Add milk, butter, nutmeg, cinnamon, and brown sugar to bowl. Mix until smooth. Fill skins with equal parts of stuffing. Place in fridge until ready to bake.

Cooking method: Oven @ 400 degrees for 30 minutes. Add mini-marshmallows and bake for another 10 minutes or until marshmallows are golden brown. Serve and enjoy!

139

NOTES

141

CAUTION: The engine will be hot, use gloves/hot pad holder when placing your lunch on the engine and when removing your lunch from the engine.

HINT: If you had chili the night before, this one is easy. Add Frito-style chips and cheddar cheese. And if not...

TIP: Follow the Almost Mama's chili recipe in the soups, salads, stews, and chili section and add Frito-style chips and cover with cheddar cheese.

FRITO PIE BURRITOS

INGREDIENTS
leftover Frito pie
12" flour tortillas

TOOLS
engine manifold
large spoon
heavy-duty foil

Camp-prep: Using leftover Frito pie, place 1 cup onto flat tortilla. Flip over each end (pick a side; its round) about 2" and then the other side. Cover ingredients and roll. Wrap tight in foil.

Cooking method: Engine block @ 190-220 degrees. One hour before ready to eat, pop the hood and place on engine manifold or intake. Unwrap and enjoy.

RV'ERS STYLE

TOOLS
microwave
large spoon
plastic wrap

Camp-prep: Using leftover Frito pie, place 1 cup onto flat tortilla. Flip over each end (pick a side; its round) about 2" and then the other side. Cover ingredients and roll. Wrap in plastic wrap.

Cooking method: Microwave on high. Heat for 1-3 minutes until hot (microwaves vary in size, so check it after 1 minute). Unwrap and enjoy.

HINT: The "Elgin Hot Sausage" can also be cut into slices and served with cheddar cheese on a cracker for a midday snack.

TIP: You will want to go home and order some more "Elgin Hot Sausage" and put them in the freezer and have them ready for your next outing.

"ELGIN HOT SAUSAGE"

OFF-ROAD & CAMPING STYLE

INGREDIENTS
leftover "Elgin Hot Sausage"
6" flour tortillas
BBQ sauce or mustard

TOOLS
engine manifold
tongs
heavy-duty foil

Camp-prep: Using leftover "Elgin Hot Sausage," place one link onto tortilla and roll up. Wrap tight in foil. Place BBQ sauce or mustard in a _____ (fill in blank) style bag.

Cooking method: Engine block @ 190-220 degrees. One hour before ready to eat, pop the hood and place on engine manifold or intake. Unwrap, put BBQ sauce or mustard on, and enjoy.

RV'ERS STYLE

TOOLS
microwave
large spoon
plastic wrap

Camp-prep: Using leftover "Elgin Hot Sausage," place one link onto tortilla and roll up. Wrap in plastic wrap.

Cooking method: Microwave on high. Heat for 1-3 minutes until hot (microwaves vary in size, so check it after 1 minute) unwrap use BBQ sauce or mustard and enjoy.

HINT: Great for hiking, fishing, canoeing, or just sitting around camp.

TIP: Try this one in a tortilla and throw it on the engine manifold or intake. Make sure that it does not interfere with the throttle linkage.

MEATLOAF SANDWICH

OFF-ROAD, CAMPING, & RV'ERS STYLE

INGREDIENTS
leftover meatloaf
white, wheat, or nut bread
mustard, ketchup, mayo

TOOLS
knife

Camp-prep: Cut meatloaf into 1/2" slices (2 per sandwich), top with your favorite condiment, and enjoy. I know, rocket science.

HINT: If you are planning on this recipe for lunch the next day, you may want to double it, because everyone may not get a No-Peek Burrito for lunch.

TIP: Use just enough gravy to cover the meat and veggies. Too much will result in a mess on your engine or in your microwave.

NO-PEEK BURRITO

INGREDIENTS
leftover no-peek stew
12" flour tortillas

TOOLS
engine manifold
large spoon
heavy-duty foil

Camp-prep: Using leftover no peek stew place 1 cup onto flat tortilla. Flip over each end (pick a side; its round) about 2" and then the other side. Cover ingredients and roll. Wrap tight in foil.

Cooking method: Engine block at 190-220 degrees. One hour before ready to eat, pop the hood and place on engine manifold or intake. Unwrap and enjoy.

RV'ERS STYLE

TOOLS
microwave
large spoon
plastic wrap

Camp-prep: Using leftover no-peek stew, place 1 cup onto flat tortilla. Flip over each end (pick a side; its round) about 2" and then the other side. Cover ingredients and roll. Wrap in plastic wrap.

Cooking method: Microwave on high. Heat for 1-3 minutes until hot (microwaves vary in size, so check it after 1 minute), unwrap and enjoy.

HINT: Change it up a little and try BBQ sauce instead of pizza sauce with chicken (precooked) as your topping. Or pesto sauce in place of pizza sauce with tomato and onion as your topping.

TIP: Make 2-3 pizzas per person, and whatever is left over, I am sure you can find someone who will be glad to take it off your hands.

MANIFOLD PIZZA ROLL

OFF-ROAD & CAMPING STYLE

INGREDIENTS
pizza sauce
pepperoni (topping choice
  pre-cooked)
grated mozzarella cheese
pita bread

TOOLS
engine manifold
small spoon
heavy-duty foil
knife

Camp-prep: Slice pita bread in half so that you have two small pizzas. Spoon small amount of pizza sauce on pita bread. Add pepperoni and then cheese. Roll jelly-roll style and wrap in foil.

Cooking method: Engine block @ 190-220 degrees. One hour before ready to eat, pop the hood and place on engine manifold or intake. Unwrap and enjoy.

RV'ERS STYLE

TOOLS
microwave
small spoon
plastic wrap

Camp-prep: Slice pita bread in half so that you have two small pizzas. Spoon small amount of pizza sauce on pita bread. Add pepperoni and then cheese. Roll jelly-roll style and wrap in plastic wrap.

Cooking method: Microwave on high. Heat for 1-3 minutes until hot (microwaves vary in size, so check it after 1 minute). Unwrap and enjoy.

Note: This is just a little of what you can do with leftovers. Be creative and come up with some of your own.

EQUIVALENT CHART

3 tsp. . . . . .1Tbsp.
2 Tbsp. . . . . .1/8 cup
4 Tbsp. . . . . .1/4 cup
8 Tbsp. . . . . .1/2 cup
16 Tbsp. . . . . .1 cup
5 Tbsp. + 1 tsp. . . . . .1/3 cup
12 Tbsp. . . . . .3/4 cup
4 oz. . . . . .1/2 cup
8 oz. . . . . .1 cup
16 oz. . . . . .1 pound
1 oz. . . . . .2 Tbsp. Fat or liquid
2 cups . . . . .1 pint
2 pints . . . . .1 quart
1 quart . . . . .4 cups
5/8 cup . . . . .1/2 cup + 2 Tbsp.
7/8 cup . . . . .3/4 cup + 2 Tbsp.
1 jigger .1 1/2 fl. Oz. (3 Tbsp.)
8 - 10 egg whites . . . . .1 cup
12 - 14 egg yolks . . . . .1 cup
1 cup unwhipped cream . . . . .2 cups whipped
1 lb. shredded cheese . . . . .4 cups
1/4 lb. crumbled blue cheese . . . . .1 cup
1 lemon . . . . .3 Tbsp. Juice
1 orange . . . . .1/3 cup juice
1 lb. unshelled wallnuts . . . . .1 1/2 - 1 3/4 cups shelled
2 cups fat . . . . .1 pounds
1 lb. butter . . . . .2 cups or 4 sticks
2 cups granulated sugar . . . . .1 pound
3 1/2 - 4 cups unsifted powder sugar . . . . .1 pound
2 1/4 cups packed brown suger . . . . .1 pound
4 cups sifted flour . . . . .1 pound
4 1/2 cups cake flour . . . . .1 pound
3 1/2 cups unsifted whole wheat flour . . . . .1 pound
4 oz. (1 - 1/4 cups) uncooked macarrón . . . . . .2 1/4 cups cooked
7 oz. spaghetti . . . . .4 cups cooked
4 oz. (1 1/2 - 2 cups) uncooked noodles . . . . .2 cups cooked
28 saltine crackers . . . . .1 cup crumbs
4 slices bread . . . . .1 cup crumbs
14 square gram crackers . . . . .1 cup crumbs
22 vanilla wafers . . . . .1 cup crumbs

153

HINT: Very rich and will go good with a big glass of milk. So whatever you do, don't forget the milk.

TIP: You can use Heath toffee chips instead of the candy bars. It makes life a little easier and you will have extra to sprinkle on top.

HEATH BAR CAKE

OFF-ROAD & CAMPING STYLE

INGREDIENTS
1 chocolate cake mix (+ ingredients
   on package)
5 Heath bars
1 jar caramel ice cream topping
1 tbsp. oil

TOOLS
dutch oven
starter fluid
charcoal
large mixing bowl
whisk

Camp-prep: Prepare cake mix according to package directions. Stir in 3 to 4 crushed Heath candy bars.

Cooking method: Dutch oven. Use 1/3 briquettes on the bottom and 2/3 briquettes on the lid. Oil dutch oven. Bake per package instructions. When finished baking, poke holes all over top of cake while hot. Pour caramel topping onto cake. Let cool. Sprinkle with remaining crushed Heath bars and serve.

RV'ERS STYLE

TOOLS
9 x 13 pan
large spoon
mixing bowl
mixer
oven @ 375 degrees

Camp-prep: Prepare cake mix according to package directions. Stir in 3 to 4 crushed Heath candy bars.

Cooking method: Oven @ 375 degrees. Bake according to package. Poke holes all over top of cake while hot. Pour caramel topping onto cake. Let cool. Sprinkle with remaining crushed Heath bars. Optional: Top individual servings with whipped topping and then sprinkle with crushed Heath bars.

HINT: If you do this one early in your camping trip, you could serve this with ice cream. Lucky RV'ers have a freezer and can have ice cream whenever they want.

TIP: Caution! This dish will be very hot and will stick to the little fingers that touch it. Please let cool 10-15 minutes before serving.

QUICK MIXED FRUIT COBBLER

OFF-ROAD & CAMPING STYLE

INGREDIENTS
1 pkg. Martha White blueberry mix
1 can (21 oz.) cherry pie filling
1 can (81/4 oz) sliced peaches, drained
2 tsp. lemon juice
1/2 tbsp. ground cinnamon
1/2 tbsp. sugar

TOOLS
dutch oven
starter fluid
charcoal
small bowl
whisk or spoon
knife

Camp-prep: In a small bowl, prepare muffin mix as directed; set aside. Cut peach slices in half.

Cooking method: Dutch oven. Use all the briquettes on the bottom to start. Combine pie filling, lemon juice, and peaches in dutch oven. Mix gently. Bring to a boil (10 minutes). Drop 6 scoops of muffin mix (space the scoops evenly apart) over hot filling, sprinkle with cinnamon and sugar. Cover and remove 2/3 of the briquettes from the bottom to the top. Continue cooking for 20 minutes, rotating every 10 minutes, until golden brown on top.

RV'ERS STYLE

TOOLS
2-qt. baking dish
small bowl
whisk or spoon
knife
oven @ 425 degrees

Camp-prep: In a small bowl, prepare muffin mix as directed, set aside. Cut peach slices in half. Combine pie filling, lemon juice, and peaches. Mix gently. Microwave in baking dish on high 3-4 minutes or until hot. Drop 6 scoops of muffin mix (space the scoops evenly apart) over hot filling, sprinkle with cinnamon and sugar.

Cooking method: Oven @ 425 degrees for 18-20 minutes or until golden brown.

157

HINT: Dressed to impress is the way I describe the Pineapple Upside-Down Cake with the array of color. It is just beautiful. (Beautiful? did I say that, ssssshhhh.)

TIP: When removing cake from the dutch oven or the skillet, I have found that by using a paper plate (which will fit inside the skillet or dutch oven), the cake will not drop on to the parchment paper. This way, if for some reason it does stick, you can turn back over and let cool a few more minutes.

PINEAPPLE UPSIDE-DOWN CAKE

OFF-ROAD & CAMPING STYLE

INGREDIENTS
4 tbsp. butter
8 pineapple rings
8 maraschino cherries
1 yellow cake mix
1 cup pineapple juice
1/3 cup water
3 eggs
1/3 cup oil
1 1/4 cups brown sugar

TOOLS
dutch oven
starter fluid
charcoal
large mixing bowl
whisk
spatula
parchment paper
hot mitts
knife

Camp-prep: In a large bowl, combine cake mix, pineapple juice, water, eggs, and oil. Mix well. Cut cherries in half.

Cooking method: Dutch oven. Use 1/3 briquettes on bottom and 2/3 briquettes on the lid. Melt butter. Evenly sprinkle brown sugar over butter (be careful not to mix). Carefully place pineapple rings on top of the brown sugar. Place cherries in center of each ring. Pour cake mix carefully over pineapple. Cook 40 minutes, rotating every 10 minutes until golden brown (center should spring back). Crack lid and cool 10 minutes. Remove lid. Place paper plate over cake. Using hot mitts, one hand on the bottom of oven and one hand on the plate. Turn oven over, holding firmly. Remove oven slowly to prevent disaster. Am I in the clouds yet?!

RV'ERS STYLE

TOOLS
9x13 cake pan
large spoon
small bowl
mixer
oven @ 375 degrees

Camp-prep: In a large bowl, combine cake mix, pineapple juice, water, eggs, and oil. Mix well. Cut cherries in half.

Cooking method: Oven @ 375 degrees. Melt butter in microwave. Evenly sprinkle brown sugar over butter (be careful not to mix). Carefully place pineapple rings on top of the brown sugar. Place cherries in rings. Pour cake mix carefully over pineapple. Cook 40 minutes, until golden brown (center should spring back). Let cool 10 minutes. Using foil, place over cake pan. Hold firmly and turn over on flat surface. Allow cake to cool. Slice and serve. Am I in the clouds yet?!

159

HINT: If you just happen to be camping (ha) and have a campfire, you can try this one in the fire. Make your Sweet Tooth Pizza and wrap it tightly in foil and toss it the fire (make sure you have tongs to flip it). 1 minute on each side. Watch the clock on this one.

TIP: Put the following in a large zipper-style bag. You are going to want to have this more than one night during your trip. Jar of peanut butter, 12-pack tortillas, bag of marshmallows, chocolate chips, container of cinnamon, and 1 cup of sugar.

SWEET TOOTH PIZZA

OFF-ROAD & CAMPING STYLE

INGREDIENTS
4-6 tbsp. peanut butter
4 flour tortillas
1/2 cup mini-marshmallows
1/4 cup semisweet chocolate chips
cinnamon
sugar

TOOLS
medium skillet
knife
camp stove

Pre-prep: Place peanut butter in a small zipper-style bag, marshmallows and chocolate chips in another zipper-style bag, cinnamon and sugar in another. Group and label.

Cooking method: Camp stove over medium/medium-high heat. Place tortilla in medium skillet. Cut bag and squeeze half of peanut butter onto tortilla. Spread with knife. Add half the marshmallows and chocolate chips. Place another tortilla on top. Cook for 2 minutes and flip. Cook for another 2 minutes (until chocolate is melted). Sprinkle with cinnamon and sugar. Cut like a pizza. Enjoy!

RV'ERS STYLE

TOOLS
medium skillet
knife
stovetop over medium/high heat

Camp-prep: Using half the peanut butter, cover one tortilla. Top with half of the marshmallows and chocolate chips. Cover with tortilla.

Cooking method: Stove top medium/med. High heat. Cook for 2 minutes and flip. Cook for another 2 minutes. (until chocolate is melted) sprinkle with cinnamon and sugar. Cut like a pizza. Enjoy!

161

HINT: Cool for about 30 minutes and serve with ice cream. This is where the RVer friend comes in, eye for an eye, tooth for a tooth, and a piece of pie for a scoop of ice cream.

TIP: Think it's good the first day? Wait till you try some the next day. This one is awesome.

CHOCOLATE PECAN PIE

INGREDIENTS
3 tbsp. butter
3/4 cups sugar
3/4 cup light corn syrup
3 eggs
1 1/2 cups whole pecans
1 cup semisweet chocolate chips
1 - 9" unbaked deep-dish pie crust

TOOLS
dutch oven
starter fluid
charcoal
whisk
knife
medium mixing bowl
camp stove
small skillet

Pre-prep: NO PRE-PREP, SORRY. But this one is well worth it. Who ever thought they could bake a fresh pie while camping? This is the Ritz.

Camp-prep: Using camp stove and small skillet, melt butter. In medium bowl, mix butter, sugar, syrup, and eggs. Blend well. Stir in pecans and chips.

Cooking method: Dutch oven. Use 1/3 briquettes on the bottom and 2/3 briquettes on the lid. Carefully place uncooked pie shell in dutch oven. Pour in mixture and cook 45 minutes (center should be firm), rotating every 15 minutes.

RV'ERS STYLE

TOOLS
foil
microwave
medium bowl
knife
oven @ 350 degrees

Camp-prep: Melt butter in microwave. In medium bowl, mix butter, sugar, syrup, and eggs. Blend well. Stir in pecans and chips. Pour in pie crust.

Cooking method: Oven @ 350 degrees. Place pie in oven on top of foil to prevent spills. Bake 45 minutes or until center is firm.

NOTES

165

HINT: The average blender is around 400 watts of power. When purchasing an inverter, make sure that it will be enough to efficiently power your blender.

TIP: DRINK, DRIVE, GO TO JAIL!

FROZEN MARGARITA

OFF-ROAD, CAMPING, & RV'ERS STYLE

INGREDIENTS
1 - 6-oz. can frozen concentrate
  limeade
6 oz. tequila
2 oz. triple sec
ice
salt

TOOLS
blender
margarita glasses
A/C inverter

Camp-prep: Fill blender 2/3 full of ice. Open limeade and pour over ice. Using the limeade container, fill it with tequila (6 oz.) and pour it in. Then take the triple sec and fill the limeade container 1/3 of the way full and pour it in. Cover and blend until smooth. Serve with or without salt. Makes four 8-oz. drinks.

Warning: These drinks are intended to be made and CON-SUMED at camp after your day's outing. **PLEASE DRINK RESPONSIBLY AND DON'T DRIVE AFTER CONSUMING ALCOHOLIC BEVERAGES. PLEASE!**

167

HINT: The breakfast that goes well with this morning-after drink is the eggs benedict topped with hollandaise sauce, but you will have to wait for *The Official Off-Road, Camping, & RV'ers Cookbook #2* to get this recipe (late November 2007).

TIP: DRUNK DRIVING, YOU CAN'T AFFORD IT!

BLOODY MARY

INGREDIENTS
1-2 shots vodka
6 oz. tomato or V-8 juice
1/2 tsp. horseradish
1 tsp. Worcestershire sauce
capful of lemon juice
2 drops Tabasco sauce
dash of pepper
celery stick
green olives
green beans
ice

TOOLS
plastic cups

Camp-prep: Combine all ingredients in cup. Stir with celery stick. Serve with celery, pickled green beans, and green olive. Great addition to your breakfast.

Warning: These drinks are intended to be made and CON-SUMED at camp after your day's outing. **PLEASE DRINK RESPONSIBLY AND DON'T DRIVE AFTER CONSUM-ING ALCOHOLIC BEVERAGES. PLEASE!**

169

HINT: This is a very tasty one and will sneak up on you quick. The recommended dose is one every twelve hours.

TIP: You will want to marinate this concoction at least 3 to 4 days and 7 days is best.

TIP: ALWAYS PRE-APPOINT A DESIGNATED DRIVER!

INFUSED VODKA

INGREDIENTS
1/2 gallon vodka
1 pint raspberries
1 pint blackberries
1 pint blueberries or 2 lb. bag frozen
  mixed berries
1 bottle Rose's blue raspberry
  infusion
ice

TOOLS
one-gallon container
plastic martini glasses
martini shaker

Pre-prep: Combine all ingredients (except Rose's blue raspberry infusion) in a one-gallon container and let sit for at least 4-5 days (7 is best).

Camp-prep: In martini shaker, use 3 parts vodka and 1 part blue raspberry mix. Fill with ice and shake, shake, shake. Faster. Pour in martini glass and enjoy. Use the berries as you would an olive in a martini.

Warning: These drinks are intended to be made and CON-SUMED at camp after your day's outing. **PLEASE DRINK RESPONSIBLY AND DON'T DRIVE AFTER CONSUMING ALCOHOLIC BEVERAGES. PLEASE!**

HINT: This is almost like a milkshake, but don't be fooled; there is alcohol in that milkshake.

TIP: IF YOU DRINK, DON'T DRIVE.

BUSHWACKER

INGREDIENTS
2 oz. vodka
2 oz. Kahlua
2 oz. Bailey's Irish cream
2 oz. amaretto
2 oz. rum
splash of milk
ice

TOOLS
plastic cups
A/C inverter
blender

Camp-prep: Fill blender 2/3 full with ice. Combine all ingredients over ice with splash of milk. Blend well until smooth. Enjoy.

Warning: These drinks are intended to be made and CONSUMED at camp after your day's outing. **PLEASE DRINK RESPONSIBLY AND DON'T DRIVE AFTER CONSUMING ALCOHOLIC BEVERAGES. PLEASE!**

HINT: Try using a pralines-and-cream style ice cream. Using a small cooler with 3-4 lbs. dry ice on top of ice cream will keep it frozen for 2-4 days, depending on the outside temperature.

TIP: DON'T BLAST OFF! IF YOU HAVE TO DRIVE OFF!

ICE CREAM BLAST

INGREDIENTS
vanilla ice cream
1/4 cup Kahlua or caramel liquor

TOOLS
spoons
plastic cups

Camp-prep: Fill glass with 2 scoops ice cream. Pour liquor over ice cream, and blast off!

Warning: These drinks are intended to be made and CONSUMED at camp after your day's outing. **PLEASE DRINK RESPONSIBLY AND DON'T DRIVE AFTER CONSUMING ALCOHOLIC BEVERAGES. PLEASE!**

Storage Times for Beef Products

Product	Refrigerator 40 °F	Freezer 0 °F
Fresh beef roast, steaks, chops, or ribs	3 to 5 days	6 to 12 months
Fresh beef liver or variety meats	1 or 2 days	3 to 4 months
Home cooked beef, soups, stews or casseroles	3 to 4 days	2 to 3 months
Store-cooked convenience meals	1 to 2 days	2 to 3 months
Cooked beef gravy or beef broth	1 or 2 days	2 to 3 months
Beef hot dogs or lunch meats, sealed in package	2 weeks (or 1 week after a "Use-By" date)	1 to 2 months
Beef hot dogs, opened package	7 days	1 to 2 months
Lunch meats, opened package	3 to 5 days	1 to 2 months
TV dinners, frozen casseroles	Keep Frozen	3 to 4 months
Canned beef products in pantry	2 to 5 years in pantry; 3 to 4 days after opening	After opening, 2 to 3 months
Jerky, commercially vacuum packaged	1 year in pantry Refrigerate 2 to 3 months	Do not freeze

Home Storage of Fresh Pork		
Product	Refrigerator 40 °F	Freezer 0 °F
Fresh pork roast, steaks, chops or ribs	3 to 5 days	4 to 6 months
Fresh pork liver or variety meats	1 to 2 days	3 to 4 months
Home cooked pork; soups, stews or casseroles	3 to 4 days	2 to 3 months
Store-cooked convenience meals	1 to 2 days	2 to 3 months
TV dinners, frozen casseroles	Keep frozen before cooking	3 to 4 months
Canned pork products in pantry	2 - 5 years in pantry; 3 - 4 days after opening	After opening, 2 to 3 months

| Refrigerator Home Storage (at 40° F or below) of Chicken Products ||
Product	Refrigerator Storage Times
Fresh Chicken, Giblets or Ground Chicken	1 to 2 days
Cooked Chicken, Leftover	3 to 4 days
Chicken Broth or Gravy	1 to 2 days
Cooked Chicken Casseroles, Dishes or Soup	3 to 4 days
Cooked Chicken Pieces, covered with broth or gravy	1 to 2 days
Cooked Chicken Nuggets, Patties	1 to 2 days
Fried Chicken	3 to 4 days
Take-Out Convenience Chicken (Rotisserie, Fried, etc.)	3 to 4 days
Restaurant Chicken Leftovers, brought immediately home in a "Doggy Bag"	3 to 4 days
Store-cooked Chicken Dinner including gravy	1 to 2 days
Chicken Salad	3 to 5 days
Deli-sliced Chicken Luncheon Meat	3 to 5 days
Chicken Luncheon Meat, sealed in package	2 weeks (but no longer than 1 week after a "sell-by" date)
Chicken Luncheon Meat, after opening	3 to 5 days
Vacuum-packed Dinners, Commercial brand with USDA seal	Unopened 2 weeks Opened 3 to 4 days
Chicken Hotdogs, unopened	2 weeks (but no longer than 1 week after a "sell-by" date)
Chicken Hotdogs, after opening	7 days
Canned Chicken Products	2 to 5 years in pantry

PROPER THAWING PROCEDURES

Uh, oh! You're home and forgot to defrost something for dinner. You grab a package of meat or chicken and use hot water to thaw it fast. But is this safe? What if you remembered to take food out of the freezer, but forgot and left the package on the counter all day while you were at work?

Neither of these situations are safe, and these methods of thawing lead to food-borne illness. Food must be kept at a safe temperature during "the big thaw." Foods are safe indefinitely while frozen. However, as soon as food begins to defrost and become warmer than 40 °F, any bacteria that may have been present before freezing can begin to multiply.

Foods should never be thawed or even stored on the counter, or defrosted in hot water. Food left above 40 °F (unrefrigerated) is not at a safe temperature. Even though the center of the package may still be frozen as it thaws on the counter, the outer layer of the food is in the "Danger Zone," between 40 and 140 °F - at temperatures where bacteria multiply rapidly.

When defrosting frozen foods, it's best to plan ahead and thaw food in the refrigerator where food will remain at a safe, constant temperature - 40 °F or below. There are 3 safe ways to defrost food: in the refrigerator, in cold water, and in the microwave.

Refrigerator Thawing Planning ahead is the key to this method because of the lengthy time involved. A large frozen item like a turkey requires at least a day (24 hours) for every 5 pounds of weight. Even small amounts of frozen food — such as a pound of ground meat or boneless chicken breasts — require a full day to thaw. When thawing foods in the refrigerator, there are several variables to take into account. * Some areas of an appliance may keep the food colder than other areas. Food placed in the coldest part will require longer defrosting time. * Food takes longer to thaw in a refrigerator set at 35 °F than one set at 40 °F. After thawing in the refrigerator, ground meat and poultry should remain useable for an additional day or two before cooking; red meat, 3 to 5 days. Foods defrosted in the refrigerator can be refrozen without cooking, although there may be some loss of quality.

Cold Water Thawing This method is faster than refrigerator thawing but requires more attention. The food must be in a leak-proof package or plastic bag. If the bag leaks, bacteria from the air or surrounding environment could be introduced into the food. Also, meat tissue can also absorb water like a sponge, resulting in a watery product. The bag should be submerged in cold tap water, changing the water every 30 minutes so it continues to thaw. Small packages of meat or poultry - about a pound - may defrost in an hour or less. A 3- to 4-pound package may take 2 to 3 hours. For whole turkeys, estimate about 30 minutes per pound. If thawed completely, the food must be cooked immediately. Foods thawed by the cold water method should be cooked before refreezing.

Microwave Thawing When microwave defrosting food, plan to cook it immediately after thawing because some areas of the food may become warm and begin to cook during microwave defrosting. Holding partially cooked food is not recommended because any bacteria present wouldn't have been destroyed and, indeed, may have reached optimal temperatures for bacteria to grow.

179

INDEX OF RECIPES

INDEX OF RECIPES

ACHIEVED DESTINATIONS

DESTINATION	DATE

FUTURE DESTINATIONS

DESTINATION	DATE

185

© 2006 Grant Reid

FAVORITE RECIPES

NAME OF RECIPE	PAGE

I have started *The Official Off-Road, Camping, & RV'ers Cookbook #2*, which will feature recipes that are a little more complex, using different spices, cooking 3-4 coarse meals, and using more than one dutch oven, but with the experience and knowledge you receive from using the first cookbook, they will be just as easy and tasty.

If you have a favorite recipe you think can be converted to cook in a dutch oven (so the off-roaders and campers can eat as well as the RV'ers) please email it to cookbook@redneckconcepts .com AND IF I DECIDE TO USE IT, WELL, YOU WILL SEE IT IN *The Official Off-Road, Camping, & RV'ers Cookbook #2* ALONG WITH YOUR NAME, CITY, AND STATE BELOW.

Thank you for purchasing my cookbook, and I hope you will have as much fun camping and cooking with this cookbook as I did writing and testing each and every recipe, so that you the cook can have "fun time" too.

See ya at camp!

Photographs were provided by:

Phillip Dayton

IPS Motorsports

Mobile/On-Site Photography

ipsmotorsports.com

Cover Design and Illustrations by:

John Falls

John Falls Design

johnfalls@nctv.com

The Official

OFFROAD

Camping & RVers

CookBook

By Grant Reid

Illustration By
John Falls

189